Southampton cooks

A taste of the world in one city

Editors: Lepsa Stojkovic, Vanessa Shahani, Cita Jagot

SOUTHAMPTON
CITY COUNCIL ®

Foreword

Welcome to Southampton Cooks, a cookery book created by the wide variety of communities that have made Southampton their home. This book has been compiled through the help of the Communities Team at Southampton City Council and the Community Involvement Team at Swaythling Housing Society.

Following the emergence of a new community known as Chapel in the inner city, and the city wide work with women from different communities, a cookery project was born. The aim of the project was to enable new and diverse communities to share their experiences and cultures through cooking. Women met on a monthly basis and cooked a dish of their choice to share with the group. These varied from family recipes to traditional national dishes.

This project led to the idea of involving more people across the city in sharing their favourite recipes by creating this book.

Southampton City Council's Communities Team and Swaythling Housing Society would like to thank the many residents who have donated their much loved recipes to this book. These recipes are representative of the culture of their country of origin and/or have been passed down through generations. We hope you enjoy them!

N.B The ingredients for many recipes can be purchased from specialist food shops across the city.

Contents

Healthy eating   5

Starters   6

Main courses   34

Salads, sauces
& dressings   102

Desserts & cakes   116

Conversion table   150

key

V	vegetarian		**tsp**	teaspoon
tbsp	tablespoon		**dsp**	dessert spoon
L	litre		**"**	inch
g	grams		**lb**	pounds
oz	ounces		**ml**	millilitres
kg	kilograms			

Healthy eating

What is healthy eating?

Getting the balance right
A healthy diet contains plenty of fruit and vegetables and starchy foods such as wholegrain bread, pasta and rice; and is low in fat (especially saturated fat), salt and sugar.

What you eat and drink can affect the process of coronary heart disease by:
• maintaining a healthy weight, reducing the strain on your heart
• lowering your blood cholesterol level
• keeping your blood pressure down
• preventing atheroma (fatty material) inside your arteries
• preventing blood clots forming.
Further information is available at:
www.bhf.org.uk

Top tips
• Eat at least five portions of fruit and vegetables every day
• Reduce the amount of fat you eat
• Eat oily fish regularly
• Reduce the amount of salt you eat
• Drink moderate amounts of alcohol: one to two units each day
• Exercise for 30 minutes at a moderate intensity on at least five days of the week
**Southampton City Council
Healthy Communities Project**

Belgian meatball soup

Belgian
Ingredients

2 large leeks
1 large onion
1 small tin of tomato purée
1 pack of pork/beef sausages

1 large head of celery
1lb packet of frozen mixed
vegetables

Method

Wash, then chop the leeks, celery and onion into small pieces.
Heat a dash of oil in a large pan.
Add the onions to the pan, cover with a lid and simmer until the
onions soften and turn clear (not browned).
Add the rest of the vegetables (including the frozen vegetables)
and season with salt and pepper - don't replace the lid.
Keep stirring for 3-4 minutes.
Add enough cold water to just cover the vegetables.
Bring the contents to the boil then reduce the heat and allow to
simmer for 1 hour - keep the lid on.
Add the meatballs - each sausage will make five balls. Split the
sausage skin, roll the sausage meat in the palm of your hands
to create your ball and pop into the pot.
Simmer for 1 & 1/2 hours, keep the lid on.
Stir in the tomato puree allowing the soup to bubble for
2-3 minutes whilst stirring.
This soup also freezes very well.

Nan Maria

6

V

Bread or buns

French Canadian

This bread recipe came from my adoptive mother's step-mother in French Canada. She made this bread every day for the family until she was well into her nineties. She would not part with the recipe and no one knew it until when she was near to dying she let her daughter send it to me.

Ingredients

Part 1

1/2 cup of margarine

1 tsp salt

3/4 cup of potato water

(with the small potato mashed in it)

1/3 cup sugar

1 small potato

2 eggs

Part 2 (mix)

1/2 cup of lukewarm water

1 tsp sugar

1 envelope of dried yeast

Part 3

4&1/2 cups of bread flour

Method

Part 1

Boil a small potato. Mash it together with the water it was boiled in (3/4 cup). Warm this water and pour over margarine, sugar and salt in a large mixing bowl. Add two eggs, well beaten.

Part 2

Mix sugar in lukewarm water. Add dried yeast, mix and soak for 10 minutes.

Part 3

Mix parts 1 and 2. Add flour. Knead well (200 times!), for about 5 minutes.

Leave to rise for about 1 & 1/2 hours, or until it has doubled in size. Knead again and place into bread tins for loaves or form into buns (rolls) and place on baking tray.

Pre-heat the oven to 180°C.

When dough has risen, put it in the oven.

Buns take about 10 minutes - loaves about 25.

When cooked brush with melted butter and pop back in oven for a couple of minutes.

You can substitute milk for potato water. Eggs can be left out if you are making loaves.

Carol

V

Cheese & wine fondue

English

This is a classic fondue recipe for four people. It is easy and quick to prepare with many of the ingredients sourced from either local, Fair Trade, British and organic sources. This makes fondue a really good sustainable dish.

Ingredients

1 clove garlic
1 tsp Fair Trade lemon juice
225g/8oz Emmental cheese
1 tsp flour
Fair Trade pepper, nutmeg and/or paprika to taste

290ml/1/2 pint (dry) Fair Trade or British organic white wine
225g/8oz Gruyère cheese
Cubed bread pieces and/or vegetables for dipping

Method

Grate the Emmental and Gruyère and combine and then sprinkle with flour.
Crush the garlic clove and rub inside of fondue pot.
Pour Fair Trade wine into pot and heat over medium heat until warm, not boiling.
Add Fair Trade lemon juice.
Add cheese by handfuls, stirring constantly with a wooden spoon until melted and cheese-wine mixture has the consistency of a creamy sauce.
Add Fair Trade pepper and nutmeg or paprika to taste.
Let boil once. Remove pot and put on lighted burner on table so fondue continues bubbling lightly.

Cut the bread and vegetables of choice into bite sized cubes and serve each guest a handful of each.
Spear fondue fork through bread or vegetable cubes.
Dunk and stir well to begin with.

To Dip
Bread cut into bite-sized cubes and/or vegetables - carrots, peppers, courgette etc.

Southampton Sustainability Forum (SSF)

To find out how to make this recipe sustainable, please check the SSF website:
www.southampton-sustainablilty.org

10

V

Gavin's nettle soup

English

Ingredients

2-3 medium sized potatoes
3 handfuls of nettles (picked carefully wearing gloves)
1 small onion
2oz butter
Vegetable stock – (2 mugs full or enough for a second helping)
Sea salt & black pepper
4 cups of water
Olive oil
Sour cream or Greek yoghurt

Method

Peel and chop the potatoes and onion. Sauté them in olive oil for a few minutes – use the same saucepan you are going to cook them in.
Next add the water with some vegetable stock and boil for 5 minutes.
Soak the nettles in water for 10 minutes, then chop them.
Add the nettles to the potatoes and stock and simmer for 10 minutes.
Add the sour cream/ yoghurt and simmer for a couple of minutes. Season to taste with salt and pepper.

Gavin

V

Hummus

Palestinian

Ingredients
400g can of chick peas (reserve a small handful for decoration if you like)
2 medium cloves garlic (1 more if they are small)
2 tbsp lemon juice (use fresh if preferred)
2 rounded tbsp tahini paste
1 tsp cumin powder
1/4 tsp chill powder (use less if want)
Salt to taste

Method
Put all the ingredients in a blender and add 1 tablespoon of water to help blend the ingredients.
Blend until smooth.
To serve spread on a plate and decorate with reserved chickpeas.
You can garnish with somak, parsley or whatever you like.
Drizzle olive oil before serving.
Eat with pitta bread.

Eman

V

Johnny cakes

African Caribbean

Ingredients
(makes 10 Johnny Cakes)
1&1/2 cups plain flour
1 tsp baking powder
1/2 tsp salt
1oz margarine
1/2 cup water
1 cup coconut oil for frying

Method
Sift flour, baking powder, salt and then rub in margarine.
Bind with water to form a soft dough (a little more water may be needed).
Divide dough into 10 balls.
Knead each one from the outside in for half a minute then fry in a pan of hot oil.
Cook gently on both sides until brown.
Drain and serve hot, split in two and spread with butter if preferred.

Gertrude

V

Kabak mücveri

(Turkish courgette fritters)

Turkish

Ingredients

1lb courgettes
1 small onion, grated
4 tbsp chopped flat-leaf parsley
4 eggs, slightly beaten
1 cup plain flour
Olive oil, for frying

1/2 cup chopped spring onions
1/2 cup chopped fresh dill
1/2 cup kasseri cheese, grated
or feta cheese, crumbled
Fresh ground pepper

Method

Grate the courgettes and place in a colander; sprinkle with salt and let drain for 30 minutes; squeeze out moisture and pat with paper towels.

Place the courgettes in a bowl and add the onions and spring onions, dill, parsley, cheese, eggs, flour and salt and pepper to taste; mix well.

In a large sauté pan over medium-high heat, pour in oil to a depth of 1/4 inch; when the oil is hot, drop the batter by heaping tablespoonfuls into the pan (or form into small patties), allow space in between fritters; fry for 2 minutes on the first side, then turn to brown on the second side for about 3 minutes; using a slotted spatula transfer to paper towels or newspaper to drain; repeat with remaining batter.

Norul

Lamb soup

Somali

Ingredients

A little oil
500g lamb meat
1 L water
3 carrots
1/2 tsp salt
Seasonings: garlic, coriander,
cardamom, to taste

2 onions
1 leek
3 potatoes
1/4 white cabbage
1/2 tsp pepper

Method

Chop the lamb into small pieces.

Peel wash and chop all the vegetables.

Put a small amount of oil into a pan, and when it is hot, add the chopped onion and fry gently until softened.

Add the lamb pieces and the chopped leek. Fry gently for 5-10 minutes stirring continuously.

Add the water, salt and pepper and seasonings and cook for 30 minutes.

Add the chopped potatoes, carrots and cabbage, and cook for a further 20 minutes until the potatoes and carrots are softened.

Yasmin

Lentil soup

Turkish

Ingredients

2 tsp olive oil
3 large cloves garlic, minced
1/2 tsp cinnamon
1/2 tsp ground ginger
1&1/4 cups dried green lentils
2 tsp chopped coriander
1&1/2 tbsp balsamic vinegar
Paprika & finely chopped
parsley for garnish

1 cup chopped onions
1 large bay leaf
1/4 tsp ground cloves
3/4 tsp ground cumin
8 cups water
1 cup chopped dried apricots
Salt & freshly ground pepper
to taste

Method

In a soup pot, heat the oil over medium-high heat. When hot, add the onions and garlic and saute until translucent. Add bay leaf, cinnamon, cloves, ginger, and cumin, and saute for about 2 minutes.

Add lentils, water, coriander, and apricots and cook for 1 hour, or until the lentils are completely soft.

Cool the soup slightly so it won't burn you, then add the vinegar. Remove bay leaf and puree soup in batches in a blender. Season with salt and plenty of pepper.

Reheat and serve hot, garnished with paprika and parsley.

Norul

Mango kerabu

Malaysian

Ingredients

350g / 5 unripe mangoes,
skin peeled & flesh shredded
20g / 1 onion, sliced
10g / 1 green chilli, diced
10g / 1 red chilli, diced
100g medium size squid
10g / 1 tbsp dried prawns, finely ground
10ml 1 tbsp vinegar
10ml / 1 tbsp lime juice
5g / 1 tsp salt
10g / 2 tsp sugar

Method

Cook the squid in boiling water and then cut into rings
Then place all the ingredients into a large bowl and mix well

Garnishing

100g cashew nut/groundnut (Toast nuts and grind finely)

Norul

V

Milk rice

Sri Lankan/Ceylon

Ingredients

1 cup basmati rice
1&1/4 cups boiling water
1/2 cup thick coconut milk
1/4 tsp salt
1 tsp butter or oil

Method

Put the rice in a strainer and wash under running water.
Drain well.
Heat butter or oil gently and add drained rice
Add salt.
Pour in boiling water.
Stir well and simmer gently on a very low heat till rice is cooked.
Add coconut milk.
Simmer for 5 minutes, stirring occasionally.
When it thickens, spoon it onto a buttered dish.
Press carefully and cut into thick pieces.

Serve with any type of curry or sweet coconut (coconut mixed with treacle and warmed).

Anusha

V

My mum's peppers

Italian

Ingredients
4 yellow peppers
4 red peppers
Pinch of salt
3-4 cloves of garlic, chopped
Olive oil – enough to cover the peppers in a jar (100-200ml)

Method
Preheat the oven to Gas mark 7 (220°C/425F).
Bake the peppers in the oven for 20-30 minutes, turning the peppers over after 15 minutes.
Take the peppers out, put them in a pot and cover with tea towel and the lid.
Save some of the pepper juices that came out whilst cooking
Slice the peppers into strips.
When they are cool enough to handle, peal the skin and core the peppers – taking the seeds out too.

Add garlic to peppers and mix. Add salt, mix.
Put the peppers in a clean jar with some of the cooking juices
Add enough olive oil to cover the peppers in a jar.

You can keep peppers in the fridge for up to 4 weeks. The longer you keep them, the stronger the flavour.
Eat with cheese, salads, meat, or just with bread.

Cathy

Pickled fish

South African

Ingredients

2&1/2 lb cod
1 tsp salt
Oil for frying
2 bay leaves
1 tsp whole peppercorns
1oz curry powder

3oz flour
1/4 tsp black pepper
1&1/2 pints vinegar
2 large onions, sliced
1oz plain flour
1 tbsp vinegar

Method

Cut the fish in slices 1 & 1/2 inches thick.
Mix flour with salt and pepper.
Roll each slice of fish in the flour mixture and shallow fry in hot oil till done. Heat the 1 & 1/2 pints of vinegar in a saucepan.
Add peppercorns, bay leaves, sliced onions and let the mixture boil. Cook until onions are soft.
Mix 1 oz of flour and curry powder with 1 tablespoon of vinegar. The mixture should look like a paste.
Add the paste to boiling vinegar, mix and cook for 2 minutes.
Arrange the cooked fish in a shallow dish and pour the vinegar sauce over.
Keep in a cold place.
You can eat the pickled fish after 48 hours.

Pileca supa (Clear chicken soup)

Serbian

Ingredients

1/2 small chicken
1 carrot cut into thin circles
Pinch of: mild curry powder, chopped basil, wild thyme (optional), chopped sage
1 tsp vegetable spice or 1 chicken stock cube
1 L water
1 clove garlic
1/4 onion
3-4 black peppercorns, 1/2 teaspoon ground black pepper
Fresh chopped parsley
Handful vermicelli pasta

Method

Put all the ingredients (except parsley and pasta) in a saucepan and cook for 30 minutes. Take the chicken out of the saucepan and break into bite size pieces. Return the chicken to saucepan. Leave it to cook for another few minutes.
Add handful of vermicelli pasta.
Add ground black pepper.
Cook for 1 minute, then turn the heat off.
Add chopped parsley.

Jelena

V

Plantains

West Indies

Ingredients

4 plantains
Water
Oil for shallow frying

Method

Put plantains into a pot and cover with boiling water.
Boil for 10 minutes until they swell and are tender.
Cut into half, then peel and cut into 4 pieces.
Fry in little oil until it gets golden brown.

Sandra

V

Crispy roasted nettles

English

It's wise to wear latex or nitrile gloves for protection while harvesting and preparing this unusual savoury snack. Cooking does remove the sting.

Ingredients
1 large bowl of young stinging nettle tips picked in spring/early summer from an unsprayed area, far from traffic fumes.
Olive oil
Tamari or soy sauce
Ground black pepper

Method
Preheat oven to Gas mark 6 (200°C/400°F).
Wash the freshly picked nettles, drain and gently remove excess moisture with kitchen towel. Place nettles in a roasting tin, one layer deep. Sprinkle generously with ground black pepper and drizzle with olive oil and Tamari or soy sauce. Still wearing gloves, toss the leaves in the tray to mix ingredients and disperse the oil so that the nettles are lightly coated. Remove gloves and place the roasting tin in the centre of your pre-heated oven for 15–20 minutes until the nettles are looking crispy and just beginning to brown.
Allow to cool and enjoy.
Nettles (Urticaria dioica) are high in nutrients and have many health enhancing properties.

Julia

V

Roti

Indian

Ingredients
2&1/2 cups medium brown flour
1 cup water
Some extra flour for dusting

Method
Add enough water to the flour so that it forms a dough. Do not add too much so that it becomes too wet.
Knead the dough until it is smooth.
Break up the dough into small pieces and roll out with a rolling pin on a floured surface.
Preheat a cast-iron pan over medium heat.
Place the rolled dough on to the pan.
When the colour changes on the top and bubbles appear, the dough will puff up, turn it over. When both sides are done remove from the pan.
Keep the roti's warm.

Suhana Group

V

Potato latkes

Russian/Jewish Serves 5-6

As Chanucah or Hanukkah falls in December, Russian Jews substituted potatoes for cheese to make latkes. It is important to allow the grated potato to drain well before use. Latkes may be served straight from the pan as a special treat; but they are also delicious instead of chips with cold meats or poultry.

Ingredients
4 large potatoes about 16floz/375 ml when grated
2 beaten eggs
4 level tbsp self-raising or plain flour
1 level tsp baking powder
1 level tsp salt
Pinch of white pepper, or to taste

Method
Grate potatoes finely.
Leave in a sieve to drain for 10 minutes.
Put in a bowl and add the remaining ingredients.
In a heavy frying pan put enough oil to come to a depth of 1/2 inch or 1cm.
When it is hot, put in tablespoons of the mixture, flattening each latke with the back of the spoon.
Cook over a steady moderate heat, for about 5 minutes on each side, until a rich brown.
Drain on Kitchen roll and serve at once.

Peter

V

Sambharo (Vegetable stir fry)

Gujarati

Ingredients
250g cabbage
3 medium size carrots
4 chillies
1/2 tsp lemon juice
1 tsp sugar
2 tsp salt
1 tsp turmeric
1 tsp mustard seeds
1 tsp asafoetida powder
1 tbsp oil

Method
Wash vegetables thoroughly.
Thinly slice carrots and chillies.
Shred cabbage.
Heat oil in a wok.
Drop in mustard seeds and when they begin to pop, add asafoetida and vegetables
Stir briskly and then add remaining spices. Simmer until the vegetables are cooked through.
Serve as a side dish or alternative to salad.

Shantaben
Suhana Group

Spring rolls

Chinese

Ingredients

Vegetarian stuffing

2 tsp oil
250g bean sprouts
700g stir-fry mixed vegetable

2 tbsp red Thai curry paste
250g finely grated carrots

Method for vegetable stuffing

Fry Thai paste in oil. Add bean sprouts, carrots, and stir fry vegetables and mix thoroughly. Continue to fry for 3 minutes. If there is too much liquid at the bottom of the pan, mix 1 teaspoon of corn flour with a little water, add to pan and stir until liquid thickens. Remove from heat.

Prawn stuffing

2 tsp of red Thai curry paste
1/3 of the fried mixture above
(vegetarian stuffing)

400g prawns

Method for prawn stuffing

Fry the Thai paste in oil and add the prawns. Mix 1 teaspoon of corn flour with a little water, add to pan and stir until liquid thickens.

To make the spring rolls:

Flour paste (for sealing spring rolls): 2 heaped table spoons of plain flour mixed with water.

Pastry (for the outside of the rolls):
You can buy either ready made spring roll pastry or ready made filo pastry (but you will need to cut each piece into a square). Once the pack is open, the pastry should be kept wrapped in a damp towel.

Wrapping the rolls
Place a spring roll wrapper in front of you so that it forms a diamond shape. Place approximately 2 tablespoons of filling near the bottom. Roll over once, fold the sides in, and then continue rolling. Seal the top with the flour paste.

Sweet & sour sauce
1/2 cup of malt vinegar
1 tsp of sugar (preferably cane molasses)
1/2 cup tomato ketchup
1/2 cup chilli sauce
Dissolve sugar and vinegar, over a low heat. Allow it to cool and add ketchup and chilli sauce. Mix well.

Jaswinder

Smoked mackerel paté

English

Ingredients
3 fillets of smoked mackerel
150-200ml natural fromage frais
Touch of red paprika

Method
Put three fillets of smoked mackerel into a blender.
Add small carton of natural fromage frais.
Add a touch of paprika if you're feeling exotic and blend.

Yes, it's as easy as that, but always fulfils.

Wendy

V

Samosas

Indian

Ingredients for the stuffing

1kg potatoes
1/2 tsp cumin seeds
Peas to taste
1 finely chopped fresh green chilli

Oil for frying
1 chopped onion
Sweetcorn to taste
Garam masala to taste

Method

Part boil the potatoes and roughly mash (keep pieces to the size of a thumb).
Fry cumin seeds in oil, add onion and cook until brown.
Add vegetables and fry until cooked.
Add potatoes, green chilli and garam masala.

Ingredients for the dough

1/2 kg plain flour & a little extra flour for dusting
Water, oil

Method

Gradually mix together water and flour until it forms a soft dough, set aside for 30 minutes. Make small dough balls (2.5cm in diameter) and put on a plate of flour. Dust each ball in flour and then roll one ball out to 15cm diameter circle. Oil it and on top of the oiled side add another rolled ball. Dust with flour and role them together to 18cm diameter. Dry fry on both sides. Separate them and keep them on a plate, covered with paper towel. (Continued on following page)

When all are done cut them in half.

Flour paste (for sealing samosas)
2 heaped tbsp of plain flour
Water
Mix well

How to fold
Put the paste on the edge, fold corner 1, and then corner 2 to mak
a cone. Fill it in with stuffing and flip the round edge over, towards
the cone's spike. Put more paste and seal the samosa. Should end
up with the triangle shape. Deep fry.

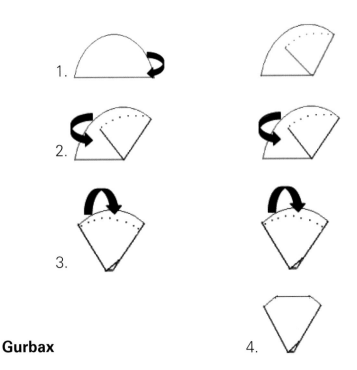

Gurbax

V

Traditional Spanish tortilla
(Omelette)
Spanish

Ingredients
1kg potatoes   3 eggs
Salt & pepper for seasoning
Oil for frying

Method
The trick is to get the egg and potato ratio right.
It should be no more than 3 eggs per 1kg of potatoes.
Peel and slice potatoes, fry them until they turn white.
Drain them, break the eggs into a mixing bowl, beat them and
then add the potatoes. Season at this stage with salt and
pepper. Use a non-stick pan, the potatoes will have absorbed
some oil so you will only need to rub the bottom of the pan with
kitchen paper that you have dipped in oil. Heat the pan to a
moderate heat.
Add the mixture and press down so as to eliminate any air
pockets. Gently reduce the heat, a little at a time, shake the pan
to release the tortilla from the pan. You can turn it using a
chopping board. Turn up the heat before returning the uncooked
side to the pan and reduce it gently as it cooks (to avoid
blackening)
If the traditional tortilla is a bit bland for the palate - buy some
chorizo and fry it gently with some mixed peppers and an onion
Add this (once sautéed) to the mixing bowl with the eggs and
potatoes and mix it in.

V

Watercress soup

English Serves 4-6

Ingredients
1 bag/500g of watercress
3 medium potatoes,
2 onions or 1 leek
1 small pot single cream (optional)
250ml of semi-skimmed milk, or more if needed
Oil for frying

Method
Chop onions or leek and sauté until they turn transparent.
Peel and chop potatoes into small cubes or slices and sauté
with onions or leek until slightly soft.
Add the watercress and sauté for 5 minutes.
Add milk and let it simmer for 15 minutes.
Make sure vegetables are covered with milk at all times. Add
more milk if needed.
Liquidise for best results.
Serve in bowls with a tablespoon of cream (optional).

Soup can be frozen and eaten at a later date.

Trees

Ackee & salt fish

African Caribbean

Ingredients

1/2 lb salted codfish
3 cups ackee flesh (red pear-shaped fruit of the ackee tree)
1/2 tsp salt
2 rashers chopped bacon
1/2 cup chopped onion
1/2 chopped tomato
1/2 chopped sweet pepper
2 tbsp oil
1 tsp black pepper

Method

Place salted codfish in enough cold water to cover.
Drain immediately. Repeat again and cover with water and bring
to the boil. Now simmer for 20 minutes until codfish is cooked.
Drain and flake fish.
Remove seeds and membranes from ackees and add the
ackees to a pan of boiling salted water (the ackees should be
well covered).
Parboil for 12-15 minutes. Drain.
Heat the oil in a frying pan and add bacon and onion. Stir.
Add remaining ingredients and sprinkle black pepper over all. Sauté
for 5-10 minutes until bacon and ackees are cooked right through.

Serve with Johnny Cake (recipe in the book page 14)

Gertrude

V

Alu dum (Potato curry)

West Bengal

Ingredients

1 tsp coriander seeds
1 tsp turmeric
1 tsp chilli powder
1lb new potatoes
1 tsp cumin seeds
Salt to taste
1 tsp cinnamon powder
Water

1 tsp whole black peppercorns
1 tsp ginger
2 tbsp plain yoghurt
Oil for frying
1 tsp sugar
1 tsp clove powder
1 tsp cardamom powder

Method

Roast coriander seeds and pepper corns in a dry frying pan.
Grind it in a pestle and mortar or in a blender.
Add turmeric, ginger, chilli powder and little water.
Add water gradually to this powder mixture to make a paste.
Add yoghurt.
Par boil the potatoes in their skins.
Peel the potatoes and coat each potato with this paste.
Heat the oil and fry cumin seeds for 1 minute.
Add the potatoes, sugar, salt and little water and cook covered till the potatoes are tender and dry.
Sprinkle with the clove, cinnamon and cardamom powder and keep covered until ready to serve.

Serve with chapattis.

Anne

Azari pilau

Azerbaijani

Ingredients

1 whole boneless chicken
– cut into small pieces
100g prunes
100g chestnuts
(cook in water for a while & clean)
1/2 tsp sugar

100g dried apricots
100g sultanas
2-5 onions (sliced)
Oil
1/2 tsp salt

Method

Fry apricots, prunes and sultanas in a little oil for 5 minutes; mix all the time so it does not burn.

Put 4-5 spoons of oil in a pot to heat.

Put layers as follows: chicken, onion, fruit and chestnuts and repeat until it is finished.

Add a glass of hot water and 4-5 tablespoons of oil. Add a little sugar and salt. Let it get to boiling point and then turn the heat down and cook slowly for 20 minutes. At the end you can stir.

Rice

For each person put 1 small cup of rice in a pot with little oil. Stir constantly on medium heat until each grain becomes white in colour (around 10 minutes). Add hot water to it to cover the rice and a bit more on top.

Turn the heat down and cook until soft.

Tamila

Babi kecap (Pork in soy sauce)

Indonesian Serves 4

Ingredients

1 onion
3 cloves garlic
1" piece ginger (peeled)
Lombok – fresh chilli (however hot you like it - my family don't let me use it)
Trasi – small amount (dash of Thai fish sauce as an alternative),
Optional
2 tbsp kecap manis
Assam (tamarind water) – use about a teaspoon of tamarind paste or a walnut sized piece of dried tamarind in half cup of hot water
750g pork (I use belly pork slices, skin removed, cut into cubes)
1 dessert spoon of sugar, preferably raw brown sugar to taste

Kecap manis is a thick sweet soy sauce available at Chinese and Asian stores. It is also very good for a base for barbecue marinades.

Method

Mince onion, garlic, ginger and chilli in a pestle and mortar or electric blender until it is a rough paste (not too smooth).
Fry paste mixture for a few minutes until it becomes cooked.
Add trasi, and then add pork cubes.
Keep frying until the meat becomes browned.
Add the kecap manis and mix thoroughly.

Add tamarind water, more water so the meat is just covered and sugar to taste.
The sharpness of the tamarind should be balanced with sweetness of the kecap and sugar.
Cook without a lid for about 1 & 1/2 hours, let the oil come out but make sure there is enough liquid to prevent sticking or burning.
Add more liquid if necessary.

Serve with plain boiled fragrant rice and steamed vegetables with gaddo gaddo (peanut) sauce.

Traditionally, Indonesian dishes are unlikely to include pork and would instead use beef or lamb. The ingredients and method for each dish are very similar however the end results in each case are quite different.

Mike

Bamya (Okra stew)

Iraqi Serves 8

Ingredients
450g/1lb diced shoulder of lamb
3 tins tomatoes
2 tbsp tomato puree
1 fluid oz lime juice
1/2 L water
500g okra, frozen
4 cloves garlic, chopped
Mint & coriander (small herb mix)
Salt & pepper to taste
Vegetable oil for frying

Method
Fry the lamb in hot vegetable oil, in a stew pot, for 2 - 3 minutes.
Add water, lime juice, tinned tomatoes, tomato puree and garlic.
Bring to the boil, and let it boil for 2 - 3 minutes then simmer for 30 - 40 minutes.
Add okra with salt and pepper and simmer for another 30 minutes, until lamb is tender.

Serve with plain basmati rice and garnish with fresh herb mix (mint and coriander).

Haider

Bariis isku koris

(Rice dish)
Somali Serves 6 people

Ingredients

1/2kg meat /shoulder of lamb
2 red onions
1 chilli
2 cloves garlic
1 tsp cumin powder
1 tsp curry powder
1-2 cardamom seeds

1&1/2 L water
1 green pepper
1 large tomato
1 stick cinnamon
1kg rice
Oil
2 chicken stock cubes

Method

Cut meat into small pieces and fry in oil. Chop 1 onion, chilli pepper, green pepper and tomato and add to pan with water. Cook for 25-30 minutes until meat becomes tender. In the meantime grind garlic and cumin powder in a pestle and mortar, and add it to the mix.
Slice the remaining onion very finely and fry in oil.
Add the cinnamon, cardamom seeds and curry powder.
Reduce heat and cook slowly.
Wash rice and add to the onion mixture. Add chicken stock cubes to the lamb and then separate the meat from the stock. Add 1 litre of the stock to the rice and bring to the boil then reduce the heat and cook slowly.
Reheat the meat in a frying pan with a bit of oil. Put the rice on a plate with the meat on top.

Amina

Beef caldereta (Beef stew)

Filipino

Ingredients

1kg beef round cut into serving pieces
2-3 cups water
1 can tomato sauce/ puree
1 cup carrots, cubed
1 cup red or green bell pepper, cut into strips
1 tsp sugar
1 cup grated edam cheese
Dash of chilli sauce

2 cloves garlic, crushed
1 cup onion, sliced
2 beef stock cubes
1/2 cup liver pate
1 cup potatoes, cubed & fried
1 tsp salt
1 tsp ground pepper
2 cups double cream
Vegetable oil

Method

Season beef with salt, add in cups of water and simmer until beef is tender. Set aside beef and beef stock.
In a separate wok, heat the vegetable oil and sauté onion and garlic until brown. Add in beef, liver pate and tomato sauce. Season with salt, pepper and sugar.
Pour in beef stock and double cream.
Simmer for 2 minutes then add carrots and fried potatoes.
Cover and simmer for another 5 minutes or until carrots are cooked. Add in grated cheese, bell pepper and chilli sauce as desired. Simmer until cheese is melted.
Serve hot with boiled rice.

Cecilia

Bobotie (Beef pie)

South African

Ingredients

1lb minced beef
1 tbsp lemon juice
1/2 cup of milk for soaking bread
2 bay leaves
1 packet/jar of ready made curry sauce

2 chopped onions
2 slices white bread
2 eggs
2 cups milk

Method

Preheat oven to Gas mark 4 (180°C/350°F).
Fry onions until soft.
Soak bread in milk and add it to the minced beef and mix well.
Add fried onions to the meat.
Add curry sauce to the meat with one cup of milk.
Add lemon juice and bay leaves.
Put the mixture into a greased dish and bake for 30 minutes.
Beat eggs with the rest of the milk.
Pour over the meat mixture and return to the oven for another 30 minutes.

Serve with rice or fresh vegetables

V

Brinju shla (Rice with spinach soup)

Kurdish

Ingredients for rice

2 cups Basmati rice
6-10 strands/individual spaghetti
3-4 cups of boiling water

4 tbsp oil
Salt to taste

Ingredients for soup

Oil for frying
3 tbsp tomato puree
Salt & pepper to taste
1/2 litre water
1 bag/ 500g spinach

1 tin chopped tomatoes,
or 4-5 fresh tomatoes
2-3 tsp of curry powder
(mild or hot)

Method for rice

Crush the spaghetti into small pieces and sauté in oil for 3 minutes.
Stir in the rice and sauté until it takes on a whitish, translucent appearance. Add salt and boiling water, mix and bring back to the boil.
Cook until all the water is absorbed.
Reduce the heat all the way down, wrap a dry dish cloth around the lid of the pan and firmly place wrapped lid on pan.
Cook for another 10-15 minutes.
When steam appears on cloth remove the pot from the hob.

Instead of spaghetti you could use sultanas and sweetcorn.
You can eat this with any type of soup.

Method for spinach soup

Heat the oil and fry the tomatoes for 5 minutes.
Add tomato puree, mix and bring it to the boil.
Add salt, pepper and curry powder, mix and add water and cook until reduced by 1/3.

At this stage you could add diced meat (chicken or lamb) which had been fried in a little oil for 10 minutes.
Leave it to boil for 10-15 minutes – the longer you cook, the tastier it will become.

Alan

Brown stew chicken

with rice and peas
African Caribbean

This is a national dish in Jamaica. The recipe was handed down to me from my dad. I like to use basmati rice but you can use brown rice.

Ingredients for Brown Stew Chicken

1 chicken skinned and cut into small pieces
All purpose seasoning
Black pepper
1/2 garlic bulb
1 medium onion
Oil for frying

Method

Place chicken in a bowl. Add crushed garlic, all purpose seasoning, onion, black pepper.
Mix the ingredients.
Leave to marinate overnight if possible. If time is limited for 1 or 2 hours. Heat a heavy bottomed pan with cooking oil. When hot add chicken piece by piece until browned.
Pour off a little oil and then replace chicken back into the pan.
Half fill the pan with water, put the lid on to keep flavours in.
Boil on a medium heat. Don't forget to add all the onions etc for flavour. Cook until the gravy has reduced and thickened slightly.

Ingredients for rice and peas

1 cup red kidney beans (If time is limited you can use tinned beans instead of dry beans)
3 cups basmati rice
6 cups of water
1/3 block of creamed coconut
1/2 small onion
2 cloves garlic
Small sprig thyme

Method

Put the kidney beans into a saucepan. Add the water and garlic (crushed), sliced onion, thyme and creamed coconut.
Bring to the boil, turn down heat and simmer.
Cook until the beans are soft.
Switch off heat. Do not throw water away as this will colour the rice. Wash the rice in cold water to wash off excess starch, and drain well. Add the rice into the kidney beans and extra water if needed to cover the rice and peas.
Bring to the boil and then turn down heat. Cover and simmer until all the water has gone and the rice and peas are cooked.

Jackie

Cabbage pallaw with meatballs

Afghani Serves 6 people

Ingredients

500g rice	750g cabbage
250g minced meat or lamb mince	1&1/2 onions
1 clove garlic	50ml oil
1/2 tsp garam masala	1 L water
1 tsp black pepper	1&1/2 heaped tsp of sugar
1 tsp coriander seeds	3&1/2 tsp salt

Method

Soak rice in water for 1 hour. Chop 1 onion preferably with julienne slice. Blend coriander seeds into fine powder (you can use coriander powder instead). Shred cabbage.

Method for the meatballs

In a blender mix together onion, garlic and mince.
Add coriander, teaspoon black pepper and a teaspoon of salt. Knead together by hand. Roll into balls. Heat a deep based frying pan with about 8 tablespoons oil. Fry balls until golden brown. Save any oil that is left.

For the cabbage pallaw

Boil the rice rapidly on high temperature for 5–8 minutes. Just before cooked drain the rice.
In the meantime heat 2 tablespoons oil in a large pan.

Slice the remaining onion and fry until golden brown.
Add sliced cabbage, and when cabbage begins to soften add an extra teaspoon of oil. Cook until the cabbage becomes dry (5 minutes). Remove from heat.
In a small pan add sugar and heat until it begins to soften and bubble. Add 2 cups of water and 2 & 1/2 heaped teaspoons of salt.
Add the remaining oil from the meat (sieve oil for best results). Remove from heat. Put rice in large pan and add 1 ladle of oil and sugar mixture. Add layer of cabbage. Add layer of meatballs. Repeat layers until all mixture has been used.
Sprinkle with garam masala. Make holes in the finished layers to allow steam to get through. Wrap a dry dish cloth around the lid of the pan and firmly place wrapped lid on pan.
Return to a high heat for 10 minutes.
When steam appears on cloth, reduce heat to simmer.
When the steam stops, turn off heat.

Serve with salad.

Samya

Cape Malay tomato bredie (Tomato and mutton stew)

South African Serves 4-6

Ingredients

750g fresh tomatoes
2 large onions, chopped
300ml hot water
3 large potatoes, peeled and sliced
10 peppercorns

2 tbsp cooking oil
1&1/2kg fatty mutton, chopped
2 tsp sugar
1 tbsp melted butter
1 tbsp flour

Method

Skin tomatoes by blanching in boiling water. Chop peeled tomatoes and set aside. Heat oil in heavy saucepan. Sweat the onions. When translucent, add mutton. Brown on all sides. Add hot water and simmer for 1 & 1/2 hours. Add sugar and peppercorns. Add tomatoes and potatoes. Cook for another 30 minutes. Thicken with a mixture of melted butter and flour and simmer for another 15 minutes. Serve with rice.

A Bredie is a Cape Malay stew. Mutton is commonly used in Malay cooking.

V

Charlie's chick peas

(Kablee Chana) and red kidney beans curry in cream
Kenyan/Indian/English

This recipe was created by experiment. Its origins can be traced back to Middle East and Asia, but this recipe was devised in Southampton.

Ingredients

2 tins chick peas
(kablee chana) drained & washed
2 onions, chopped
1 tbsp dried oregano
1 tsp red chilli powder
1/2 tsp turmeric powder
1 tin chopped tomatoes
3 tbsp balsamic vinegar

1 tin red kidney beans
(drained & washed)
4 cloves garlic, chopped
1 tsp salt
140ml single cream
1 tbsp brown sugar
100g tomato puree
100ml olive oil

Method

Use a medium sized pot. Pour in oil and heat till the oil gets a bit smoky. Add the chopped onion, garlic and fry till soft. Then add the dried oregano, salt, chilli, turmeric powder and fry for two minutes. Add balsamic vinegar and brown sugar and fry for 1 minute. Add the tinned tomatoes and the tomato puree and fry for 5 minutes. Add the chick peas (Kablee Chana) and then the red kidney beans, and cook for 15 minutes on a medium heat. Add the single cream and stir well and then cook for another 10 minutes on a low heat.
Enjoy with Naan bread or rice!

Chicken charttinad

The famous black peppercorns of South India make this chicken delicacy a hot favourite and give it a special flavour of star anise.

Indian Serves 3 people

Ingredients

1.2kg chicken breast
1 tbsp coriander leaves
1 tbsp garlic
1 tbsp ginger
180g onions chopped
160g tinned tomatoes
1 tsp turmeric powder
1 tsp red chilli whole
Parsley (for garnish)
3 small green cardamoms
1 cinnamon stick

1 tbsp black peppercorns
1 tsp garam masala
60ml oil
1 tbsp salt
40g coconut powder
1 tsp chilli powder
1 tsp star anise
10 curry leaves
2 large black cardamoms
2-3 bay leaves

Method

Cut the chicken, wash with cold water, drain, put to one side. Chop onions. Make paste of garlic and ginger with red chilli powder, salt, turmeric powder and garam masala.
Heat oil in a deep pot, add star anise, red chilli whole, big and small cardamoms, cinnamon stick, bay leaves and curry leaves. Let it crackle, then add chopped onions, cook until golden brown. Add garlic and ginger paste, blended tomatoes, cook until oil comes to the surface. Add coconut powder, cook for 10 minutes. Add washed chicken, heat until chicken is well cooked. Remove from heat and serve, garnish with curry leaves, fried red chilli and parsley.

Chef Saifuddin Mohammed, Kuti's Brasserie

Chicken curry

Indian Cooking time: 45 minutes

Ingredients

4 medium onions

1" ginger

1 tbsp garam masala

1 tin coconut milk

4 chicken fillets (1 per person)

Fresh coriander

2 cups of water

4 cloves of garlic

3 green chillies

1 tsp coriander powder

2 tins chopped tomatoes

2 level tbsp salt

Oil for frying

Method

Put a small amount of oil in a pan. Chop the onions and add to pan, let the onion simmer until soft, be careful not to burn. Chop the garlic and add to onions in the pan. Add the tins of tomatoes. Add the ginger. Let it all simmer for about 20 minutes. Use a hand blender to blend the contents of the pan together. Let it brown. Add the coriander powder and the garam masala Add the coconut milk. Simmer for about 10 minutes. Add the chicken and let it brown (if you prefer you can brown the chicken in a different pan and then add).

Once the chicken is cooked, add two cups of water and then let it simmer. Chop the fresh coriander and add to garnish once the curry is cooked.

This recipe can also be cooked with lamb or vegetables; if cooking with vegetables steam the vegetables before adding them to the curry.

Satveer

Come and enjoy gourmet Indian dining

ENTERPRISING RESTAURATEUR Miff is building on the success of his innovative Winchester venture by expanding into the heart of Southampton's quality dining district – Oxford Street.

Miff's Tiffin Club has established a reputation for creative cuisine with dishes such as Wild Hampshire Venison, Broughton Water Buffalo Bhoona and an extensive fish range including Barramundi, Monkfish and Lobster. This reputation has spread to the Indian Cricket team who dined here recently.

"I love food! I have such fun devising new dishes and challenging taste buds and preconceptions" says Miff, winner of the 1999 national BBC Mega-chef award. The adventurous amongst are recommended to try the ZYAVA, a dark eclectic mix of chocolate, tamarind and chilli which thrills the taste buds.

The focus on taste and quality is exemplified by the choice of the finest Hampshire ingredients – fresh, organic and local produce are selected to complement Indian spices and cooking techniques for a delectable dining experience.

There is a an extensive and varied selection for vegetaria such as the fresh and nutty Asparagus and Sesame or t mildly delicious Sweet Potato and Coconut Milk.

The Tiffin Club team look forward to welcoming you to the fabulously stylish new restaurant that Southampton can be proud of.

Tendulkar and the Tiffin Te

A warm welcome awaits you

Chicken Dhansak

Indian

Ingredients

Bunch of fresh coriander
3 cloves garlic
1 tsp garam masala
175g moong dahl
675g jointed chicken legs/thighs
225g spinach

2 large onions
1 tsp ground ginger
175g channa dahl
175g butter or oil
2 large tomatoes
3/4 litre chicken stock

Method

Wash and rinse all dahls and cover with stock and simmer until soft. Slice onions, fry for 5 minutes then add crushed garlic, ginger and masala. Add chicken and brown (but don't burn!) Chop tomatoes and spinach and add to pot - cook for 10 minutes. Mash the cooked lentils and add to pot. Cover and cook on low heat until chicken falls off the bone.
Chop coriander and add at last minute and serve.

Pete

V

Cook-up rice

Guyanese Serves 6-8

Ingredients

2 cups Fair Trade brown basmati rice
5 cups liquid coconut milk and water* (see method on next page)
1 large onion chopped
1x 400g tin Fair Trade aduki, or black beans – drained
1 tbsp (or to taste) chopped fresh basil
1 tsp fresh or dried thyme
Salt & pepper to taste
Chilli to taste
Cooked chicken, beef, or salt beef – optional
A few spinach leaves, and about 6 okras

Method

Heat liquid. Add all other ingredients except spinach and okras.
Reduce heat and simmer for about 30-35 minutes or until rice is
cooked and liquid evaporates. Stir regularly. Add okras and
roughly chopped spinach leaves. Cook for another 2-3
minutes. If liquid evaporates and rice is not fully cooked, add a
small amount of hot regular milk and continue to cook. If meat
is not used, cookup can be served with fried fish. This dish can
be cooked in a pressure cooker. Cook for about 12 minutes.
Add spinach and okra afterwards. Leftovers can be frozen.

*To make fresh coconut milk

Ingredients
1 Fair Trade coconut
2 cups water
A hand grater or a blender
A sieve

Method
Break coconut.
Scoop the white flesh out, wash and cut into small pieces
Place in a blender with the water and blend for about 3 minutes on medium speed.
Pour into a sieve and squeeze over a large bowl.
Discard the coconut husk.

Coconut milk can be kept in refrigerator for a couple of days or frozen for use later.

Amna

Corned beef hash

English

Ingredients
1 tin 500g corned beef hash
1 clove garlic, crushed
1 onion, chopped
Tomato paste
2 large mushrooms chopped
1/2 cup stock
3 large potatoes
Grated cheese to sprinkle on top
Black pepper to taste
Pinch chilli powder

Method
Pre-heat oven to Gas mark 7 (425°F/220°C).
Fry garlic, mushrooms and onion and season with black pepper and a small pinch of chilli powder.
Add corned beef and stir continuously until turning brown.
Add tomato paste and stock.
Cook until most of the liquid is gone and then turn off heat.
Boil and mash the potatoes.
Put hash into a dish, cover with mashed potato and sprinkle with grated cheese.
Bake in oven until cheese bubbles and browns.
Serve with fresh bread.

Bev

Chicken with green pepper in black bean sauce

Chinese

Ingredients

200g diced chicken
1 diced green pepper
1/2 tbsp crushed garlic
1/2 tbsp corn flour
(mix into a paste with little water)
1 tsp oil

1 small diced onion
1/2 tbsp black bean sauce
1/4 cup of water
Pinch of salt
1&1/2 tsp sugar
Few drops of dark soy sauce

Method

Heat the wok with the oil.
Once the wok is hot, add the garlic, onion and green pepper
Stir for 1 minute.
Add the chicken and stir for another minute.
Add the 1/4 cup of water and cook for 2-3 minutes.
Add the black bean sauce and stir for 1 minute.
Add the salt and sugar and then stir in the corn flour mixed with water, to thicken the sauce.
To add colour – add a few drops of soy sauce.

Serve with boiled rice.

Amy

Cawl

Welsh

This is a traditional Welsh meat broth with veggies, a great winter warmer!

Ingredients

1lb neck fillet of lamb
2 large leeks
1 small swede or turnip
1oz parsley

1/2lb of carrots
1/2oz corn flour
1lb potatoes
Salt & pepper

Method

Slice meat and put into saucepan, cover with cold water, add pinch of salt and pepper and bring to the boil.
Skim surface to remove excess fat (if done night before fat will set on surface so easier to skim).
Add carrots (cut in half) swede (sliced) and leeks (sliced).
Simmer gently for 2 & 1/2 hours.
Add potatoes and simmer for another 30 minutes.
When potatoes are nearly cooked through add flour and a little water.
Add parsley, simmer for another 10 minutes.
Serve with warm crusty bread and Caerphilly cheese – delish!

Rhys

V

Daal

Pakistani

Ingredients

2 cups red lentils
1 chopped onion
20 whole black peppercorns
1 tsp chilli powder (or to taste)
4 black cardamom pods
1 tsp salt
Enough water to cover
the lentils

2 tbsp oil
2 tsp cumin
10 cloves
Pinch ground turmeric
1 tsp garlic & ginger paste
(you can buy, or make your
own by mixing crushed garlic &
ginger together)

Method

Soak the lentils in water for 10 minutes.
Heat the oil in a pan. Add the onion and fry until browned (put
some aside for garnish). Add cumin, then peppercorns and
cloves. Add chilli powder. Fry together for 3 minutes
Add lentils. Add turmeric and black cardamom pods.
Mix together and add garlic and ginger paste, and salt to taste
Cover lentils with water and bring to the boil. Cover and
simmer on a low heat until all water has been absorbed.
Garnish with sliced green chillies and browned onion.

You can use it as a main course with rice or a side dish with
any curry.

Arzoo

V

Dahl dhokli

Indian
Cooked in 3 steps: first cook dahl, add the tempering mixture to the dahl and then add dhokli to dahl.

Ingredients for dahl

200g tuver dahl
3-4 cups of water
(to be used when dahl is added
to tempering mixture)
2 tbsp sugar
Green chillies, diced

3 cups of water
1 tsp garam masala
1 tsp salt
1tsp turmeric
2&1/2cm fresh ginger shredded
1 tsp lemon juice

Method for cooking dahl

Wash dahl 2-3 times in warm water. Put dahl into pressure cooker or a deep saucepan. Add water and all the other ingredients. Cook until done. Drain and set aside.

Ingredients for the tempering
(adding spices to the cooked dhal)

2 tbsp oil
5 cloves
1tsp fenugreek seeds
Pinch of asafoetida
(Arabic gum powder)
(optional)
1 tbsp shredded coconut

4 small cinnamon sticks
1 tsp mustard seeds
1/4 tsp cumin seeds
10-12 curry leaves(optional)
1 tin chopped tomatoes
5-6 lemon slices
2 Coriander leaves for garnish

Method for tempering

Put oil in a pot. Add cinnamon sticks and cloves.

When cinnamon and cloves start crackling add mustard seeds, fenugreek seeds, cumin seeds, asafoetida, curry leaves and tomatoes.

When the oil separates from the tomatoes, add the cooked dahl.

Add 3-4 cups of water and when it boils add pieces of dhokli gradually and stir.

Cook 10-15 minutes on medium heat.

Sprinkle with coconut and coriander leaves, and serve with lemon slices.

Ingredients for Dhokli dough (dumplings):

2 cups flour & some extra for dusting
1 tsp dry coriander powder
1 tsp caraway seeds
1 tbsp coriander finely chopped

1/2 tsp turmeric powder
1/2 tsp salt, or to taste
1 tsp red chilli powder
1-2 tbsp oil
Warm water for dough

Method for Dhokli

Mix all the ingredients together, except water.

Start adding lukewarm water and knead into a hard dough.

Make 12-15 balls of the dough. Roll each ball with a rolling pin into thin rotis, dusting with flour if necessary. With scissors shape each piece into square.

Roast slightly in a skillet on both sides, until the rotis dry up slightly.

Jamnaben, Suhana Group

Goan cod curry

Goan style cod fish cooked in onion tomato and coconut milk, served with basmati rice.

Serves 4 people Cooking time 40 minutes

Ingredients for gravy

500g onion
300g plum tomatoes
1 tsp curry leaves
2 tsp garam masala
1 tsp turmeric powder
1 tbsp mustard oil
2 tsp ginger paste

1/2 tsp chilli flakes
100g coconut milk
1/2 tsp mustard seeds
2 tsp red chilli powder
2 tsp salt
2 tsp garlic paste

Method for gravy

Peel onions and chop finely. Chop tomatoes finely.
Add oil to a pot, heat, then add mustard seeds, curry leaves and chopped onions, cook till golden brown. Make paste of ginger and garlic with red chilli powder, turmeric powder, salt and garam masala. Add to pot, cook for 4 minutes. Add chopped tomatoes and cook until oil is left on surface. Add coconut milk, cook for another 10 minutes.

Ingredients for cod

1 cod fillet
1/2 tsp chilli flakes
1/2 garlic paste
1/2 tsp turmeric powder

1/2 cup gram flour
1/2 tsp ginger paste
1/2 tsp salt
1 tbsp lemon juice

Method for cod
Remove all bones from fish, cut into 4 rectangular sizes.

Batter for cod
Add flour to a bowl, chilli flakes, ginger and garlic paste, salt, turmeric powder and a little lemon juice.
Coat the cod with the batter then deep fry at 160°C.
Add cod to gravy for 5 minutes.
Serve with basmati rice.

Chef Peter Moiley Gomes, Kuti's

Green bananas, steamed dumplings & dried spicy cod

African Caribbean

Ingredients

4 large green bananas
1 oz margarine
1 tbsp mixed herbs
400g dried salted cod
3 cloves garlic crushed
2 tbsp corn flour
1 bunch Callalo
(washed and finely stripped)
Oil for frying

6 oz self raising flour
Salt to taste
1 Scotch bonett pepper
(remove seeds)
1 medium size onion
finely chopped
1 cup of water
1tbsp paprika

Method

Cod: Soak cod to remove the salt. Boil for about 15 minutes
Remove the skin and bones. Flake the cod and set aside. Next heat
2 tablespoons of oil in a pan and add onion and garlic. Keep stirring
on a low heat for about 10 minutes. Add cod, pepper, 1 teaspoon
mixed herbs and 1 teaspoon paprika and stir. Mix a little water to
the corn flour and then add to the cod. Stir until the sauce thickens.
Remove bonett pepper before serving.
Dumplings: Sift flour and salt and rub in margarine. Add 2
teaspoons herbs and water and make a dough. Make 8 dumplings
and steam until cooked. Steam Callalo for 20 minutes.
Bananas: Boil bananas unpeeled for about 20 minutes.
When cooked, remove the skin and clean bananas.

Dottie

Green lentils & carrots

French Serves 4
This used to be my favourite dish when I was little (and still is!)
It has now become my little boy's favourite too!

Ingredients
500g green lentils
3 carrots
3 bay leaves
1 celery stick

1 onion, sliced
200g bacon rashers, sliced
A few twigs of parsley

Method
Fry the onion and bacon in a large non stick pan.
Rinse the lentils. Add to the pan with the carrots and herbs.
Cover with water and bring to the boil. Simmer for
approximately 1 hour, or until the lentils are cooked (add water if
necessary). When cooked, add salt and pepper to taste.

Virginie

Haggis

Scottish

Ingredients

Set of sheep's heart, lungs, liver
& intestines (cleaned by a butcher)
1 cup medium ground oatmeal
1 cup beef stock
1 tsp salt & tsp pepper

1 beef bung (intestine)
3 cups finely chopped suet
2 medium onions
1/2 tsp mace
1 tsp nutmeg

Method

Trim off any excess fat and sinew from the sheep's intestine
and, if present, discard the windpipe. Place in a large pan, cover
with water and bring to the boil. Reduce the heat and simmer
for an hour or until they are all tender. Drain and cool. Toast the
oatmeal in an oven until it is thoroughly dried out, but not
browned or burnt. Finely chop the meat and combine in a large
bowl with the suet, oatmeal, finely chopped onions, beef stock,
salt, pepper, nutmeg and mace. Make sure the ingredients are
mixed well. Stuff the meat and spices mixture into the beef
bung which should be over half full. Then press out the air and
tie the open ends tightly with string. Make sure that you leave
room for the mixture to expand or else it may burst while
cooking. If it looks as though it may do that, prick with a sharp
needle to reduce the pressure. Place in a pot and cover with
water. Bring to the boil and immediately reduce the heat and
simmer, covered, for 3 hours. Avoid boiling vigorously to avoid
bursting the skin. Serve hot with "champit tatties and bashit
neeps" (mashed/creamed potato and turnip/swede). You can
pour a little whisky over the haggis. Don't go overboard on this
or you'll make the haggis cold.

Shakira

Heavenly chicken
(Chinese stewed chicken)
Chinese Serves 3-4

This home recipe, called by my son's friends the heavenly chicken, is an all time success when I have guests, old or young, Chinese or non-Chinese. It is not only authentic but also very simple to do.

Ingredients

6 chicken thighs or drumsticks
2 tbsp dark soy sauce
1 tbsp brown sugar
2 spring onions,
chopped into 4/5cm long pieces
1or 2 tsp salt, according to taste

2 whole star anise
2 tbsp light soy sauce
1" root ginger, pealed &
thinly sliced
250ml water

Method

Put the dark and light soy sauce into a medium sized saucepan, add the star anise, sugar and ginger and cook on medium heat for about one minute. Add the water, and cook on medium heat till it boils. Put the chicken in and add salt. Cook on high heat till it boils. Turn the heat down, cover with lid and cook for 30 minutes. Stir once or twice during that time to make sure the sauce stays juicy.
Add the spring onion. Remove the lid and cook until the sauce becomes thick. Eat with rice or noodles.

Yan

Irio

Kenyan Serves 6-8

Irio is a Kikuyu Speciality dish (one of the biggest tribes in Kenya)

Ingredients

3 lb potatoes, peeled & quartered
2 white onions, finely chopped
1 lb garden peas
1 lb sweetcorn (tinned)
2 cloves garlic, chopped
2 pints chicken stock
1/2 stick butter
1/2 tsp salt & pepper

2lb fresh long leaf spinach, chopped including the stalks (or 2x10 oz packets of frozen chopped spinach)
1/2 pint sour cream (optional)

Method

Finely chop the onion and garlic and sauté in some butter until soft. Add the chopped spinach, potatoes, peas and sweetcorn. Sauté everything in butter for about 12 minutes. Now add the chicken stock and simmer for approximately 25 minutes, or until potatoes are soft. Drain excess stock. Use a potato masher to mash everything until it has the consistency of lumpy mash, with some of the peas and corn left intact. Now add the sour cream. Use salt, pepper and nutmeg to taste.

Jerk pork

African Caribbean Serves 8-10

Ingredients
4 & 1/2 lb shoulder of pork
1 tbsp all spice
1/2 tsp cinnamon
1/4 cup chopped scallion
3 tbsp salt
2 sprigs thyme

2 tsp finely chopped hot peppers
1/2 tsp grated nutmeg
1 tbsp minced garlic
1/4 cup chopped onions
2 tbsp black pepper

1/2 cup oil
3/4 cup crushed dry pimento leaves
1 cup water

Method
Wipe pork well. Mix the next ten ingredients together and rub
well into the pork. Leave it covered over night in the refrigerator.
Heat the oil in a thick bottomed saucepan.
Fry pork for 10 minutes. Turn pork and add the water and
crushed pimento leaves and cook slowly 1 & 1/2 - 2 hours
Turn from time to time.
When cooked chop the meat into pieces and bake at 400°F for
10 minutes to dry it out before serving.

N.B. Ask your butcher to chop the meat
through the bone several times,
but kept in one piece.

Gertrude

Ladoupe poule

(Chicken)
Mauritian

Ingredients
1/2 large onion
1"ginger
1 sprig coriander
8 thighs/legs chicken
(any part depending
on preference)

3 cloves garlic
1 chilli (or to taste)
1/2 tin chopped tomatoes
3 potatoes chopped into
quarters
1/4 tsp thyme

Method
Fry onions and then add garlic and ginger (finely chopped).
Fry gently for a few minutes, be careful not to burn garlic.
Add some chilli and then add the meat.
After 15 minutes add half a tin of chopped tomatoes and
chopped potatoes.
Allow to simmer for 25 minutes. Add thyme, and salt to taste.
Before serving add coriander to garnish.

Shelina

Lagan ki bathak

Pot roasted duck fillet simmered in poppy seeds, melon seeds, coconut, yogurt and exotic spices. Serve with pilau rice.

Serves 4 people Cooking time 30 minutes

Ingredients

4 duck fillets
1 tsp garlic
1/2 tsp coriander powder
1/2 tsp turmeric powder
2 tsp white poppy seeds
2 tsp melon seeds
1/2 tsp peppercorns
3 green cardamoms
30 ml oil

1 tsp ginger
2 tsp mustard oil
1/4 tsp garam masala
50g plain yogurt
2 tsp desiccated coconut
100g onions
1 cinnamon stick
1 black cardamom

Method

Duck marination: Clean the duck fillets. Slash the skin so the marinade can soak into the meat. Mix salt, chilli powder, turmeric, ginger, garlic and mustard oil, together then marinade meat. Put to one side for 30 minutes. Heat oven to Gas mark 3 (160°C/325°F). **Gravy:** Chop the onions finely, put to one side. Roast the coconut, melon and poppy seeds in a wok and blend with a little water. Heat oil in deep pan, add the cardamoms and cinnamon, let them crackle. Add chopped onions cook till golden brown, add ginger, garlic, turmeric powder, red chilli powder, coriander powder and cook for 3 minutes. Add yogurt, cook for a further 10 minutes, add the roasted paste and cook until oil floats on the surface. Place the marinated breast in the oven for 12-14 minutes at 160°C. Serve with rice.

Chef Sad Miah, Kuti's Brasserie

Lal mans

Serves 4 people Cooking time 45 minutes

A delicacy of Rajputs, tender lamb chops cooked in onions and tomato puree, smoked with exotic spices in a sealed pot and served with aloo pitika.

Ingredients

16 lamb chops
100g tomato puree
1 tsp salt
2 small cardamoms
1 black cardamom
20ml oil
1 tsp ginger
1 tsp cummin seeds
Dutch chilli (garnish)

200g onions
2 tsp deghi mirch
1 clove
2 cinnamon sticks
1/4 tsp peppercorns
50g mash potatoes
1 tsp garlic
Spring onions (garnish)
2 bay leaves

Method

Heat oil in deep pot. Add small and big cardamom, cinnamon stick, bay leaves, clove and peppercorns, let them crackle. Add sliced onion, cook until golden fried. Add ginger and garlic paste with deghi mirch. Add little water so the onions will soften, add the lamb chops and cook for 10 minutes. Add water every few minutes to make the paste of gravy, add tomato puree and heat until the lamb chops are cooked. To serve, add salt, red chilli fried, coriander fresh, coriander seeds and cummin seeds to mash potato. Use bowl dish, mould the mash potato into a pastry cutter, remove cutter to leave small potato mound, add sauce around the base of potato. Add the lamb chops and garnish with spring onions and dutch chilli.

Chef Mukesh Sharma, Kuti's

Lamb curry

Pakistani

Ingredients

2kg diced lamb
4-5 onions chopped
4 tsp ground coriander
10 black peppercorns
5 heaped tbsp of
natural yogurt

6 tsp oil
1 & 1/2 tsp chilli powder
4 tsp garlic & ginger paste
5-6 whole cardamom seeds
6 cloves
Salt & pepper to taste

Method

Heat the oil in a deep pan.
Fry the chopped onions until browned.
Add chilli powder, ground coriander, garlic and ginger paste.
Add lamb and fry until browned.
Add a little water to make a paste.
Add cardamom seeds (crack them slightly open first).
Add peppercorns and cloves.
Simmer for 10 minutes to tenderise the meat.
In a bowl stir in 5 tablespoons natural yogurt and beat well (to avoid lumps forming).
Add yogurt to the rest of ingredients.
Simmer on low heat.

Serve with rice or lentils.

Arzoo

V

Lemon rice

Southern India

Ingredients

1kg cooked rice
1 tbsp mustard seeds
4 whole dry red chillies
(seeds removed)
3 tbsp sultanas
Salt to taste
Oil for frying

2 tbsp olive oil
1 tbsp split lentils
150g cashew nuts
1 tsp turmeric
Juice of 1-3 lemons
Handful of chopped coriander

Method

Heat oil in a pan.
Add mustard seeds and let it splutter.
Add split lentils and chillies.
Fry until brown.
In a separate pan, gently fry cashew nuts and add to above
ingredients.
Add sultanas.
Add turmeric and salt to taste.
Add lemon juice according to taste.
Take off heat.
Pour over rice and mix with hands.
Sprinkle with chopped coriander.

Veena

V

Lentil bake

English Serves 4

Ingredients

1 cup lentils
2 medium onions, chopped
Pinch of thyme
2 tbsp tomato ketchup
Oil for frying

2 eggs
6 oz grated cheese
Salt & pepper to taste
2 tbsp breadcrumbs

Method

Preheat the oven to Gas mark 4 (180°C/350°F).
Cook lentils for 20 minutes.
Whilst hot, add 4 oz grated cheese.
Fry the onions until golden.
Add seasoning and ketchup and mix.
Add eggs and mix well.
Transfer into 8 inch baking dish.
Sprinkle with remaining cheese.
Sprinkle breadcrumbs on top.
Bake for 30-45 minutes, until crispy on top.

Kirsten

V

Ma Pascoe's Cornish pasties

Cornish/English Recipe for each pasty (1 person)
You can make these with beef steak, lamb steak or just vegetables!

Ingredients

4 oz short crust pastry
1 small onion, chopped
Seasoning to taste
2 tbsp of meat or veg stock

2 medium size potatoes, sliced
(any other chopped vegetables
if making a vegetarian pasty)
1 egg - beaten

Method

Short crust pastry

You can buy short crust pastry or make your own as follows:
4 ounces of plain flour in a bowl. Add 1 ounce of margarine,
pinch of salt. Mix together with a little water. Roll the pastry into
a 7 inch across circle.

Filling

Thinly slice potatoes and lay most on pastry. Chop onions and
place on potatoes. Add meat cut into small cubes (add other
sliced vegetables if vegetarian pasty). Add remainder of sliced
potatoes on top. Season, including herbs if you fancy. Coriander,
yum! Add two dessert spoons of stock (optional). Damp the
inside edge of the pastry. Pull two opposite sides together, roll
and squeeze edges. Crimp the edge between your fingers.
Brush pastry with a little beaten egg.

Cooking

Place on baking tray in a preheated oven.
Gas mark 7 (220°C/ 425°F) for 15 minutes then turn temperature
to Gas mark 4 (180°C/350°F) for 30 minutes.

Tony

Mincemeat curry

Pakistani Serves 4

Mincemeat curry is an easy and quick curry. My dad passed it to me. My older son enjoys eating this curry. It can be served with chapatti and rice. Go on try it!

Ingredients

2 lb Mincemeat lamb or beef
1 tsp ginger
1 tomato
1/2 tsp chilli powder
1/2 tsp coriander powder
1/2 tsp turmeric powder

2 onions
1 tsp garlic
2 tbsp oil
1/2 tsp salt
1/2 tsp cumin powder

Method

Chop onions finely and fry with garlic and ginger until golden brown. Add mince and rest of ingredients and cook for 20-30 minutes until mince is cooked. Add the rest of the spices.
If you want you can add potatoes or peas and cook for a further 15 minutes.

Mabushra

V

Miss Victoria's healthy vegetarian lasagne

English

Ingredients for the vegetable sauce

1 courgette
1 yellow pepper
20 button mushrooms
2 tbsp olive oil
2 tins chopped tomatoes

1 red pepper
1 red onion
1-2 cloves garlic
1 tsp mixed italian herbs
2 tbsp concentrated
tomato puree

Note: you can add any vegetables you like and I often add sweetcorn, sun dried tomatoes etc. The only vegetables I wouldn't put in are starchy ones such as potatoes.

Ingredients for the white sauce

1 & 1/2 pints of UHT
skimmed milk
1 tsp dijon mustard

2 tbsp vegetable oil
2 tbsp plain flour
Salt & pepper to taste

Lasagne Sheets – green or white
A little grated cheese of your choice to sprinkle on top.

Preheat oven to Gas mark 4 (180°C/350°F).

Method

Chop the onion and fry in the oil.
When it is nearly softened add the garlic. Then add all the vegetables which you have cut into inch squares. Fry this lightly

and then add the two tins of chopped tomatoes.

Heat throughout and then turn off the heat and put to the side.

For the sauce start off by gently heating the oil, take off the heat and add flour to the oil, as much as you can until you have a thick paste. Then return to the heat and add the milk.

Bring to a simmering point gently which whisking to get rid of any lumps. When the sauce starts to thicken (about 10mins) add the Dijon mustard and salt and pepper. Continue to heat and taste the sauce until you can no longer taste the flour (about 20mins in total). Then turn off the heat and put to the side.

You now have to put it all together! You need to layer the ingredients as follows:

Vegetables / Pasta / White sauce / Pasta / Vegetables / Pasta White Sauce.

You finish with the white sauce and then sprinkle with grated cheese and pop into a pre-heated oven at Gas mark 4. (180°C/350°F) for approximately 30 minutes. You can check that the lasagne is cooked by inserting a knife through the pasta. If the pasta isn't cooked and it is already brown on top then just pop some foil over it and continue to cook until the pasta is al dente'

Vicky

V

Mixed vegetable curry

Indian

Ingredients

250g runner beans, chopped
2 medium sized potatoes,
peeled and diced
1 tsp hing/asafoetida powder
Handful chopped coriander
to garnish
2 tsp haldi/turmeric powder

1 medium aubergine, chopped
3 tbsp oil
2 tbsp cumin powder
Salt to taste
1 tbsp mustard seeds
1 tbsp cumin seeds
1 tbsp red chilli powder,
or to taste

Method

Heat oil, add mustard seeds, cumin seeds and hing powder.
Add runner beans, aubergine, potato, salt and haldi and cook
for 10 minutes. Add tomato and coriander and cook for a further
10 minutes. At the end of cooking add in cumin powder and red
chilli powder.
Serve with rice or chapatti.

Suhana Group

Muckloobah

Palestinian

Ingredients

8 pieces of chicken or lamb
1 big aubergine
1 cauliflower
1-2 L water
2 cups of rice – washed, soaked in cold water
1 onion chopped
1/2 tsp curry powder
1/2 tsp coriander powder

2 cloves of garlic
4-5 potatoes
1 courgette
Vegetable oil
2 green chillies
1 onion, sliced
2-3 sage leaves
1/2 tsp cumin powder
2 cups chicken/lamb stock

Method

Boil chicken or lamb until half cooked, adding 2 cloves of garlic and 1 sliced onion to the water. Add sage, curry powder, cumin powder, and coriander powder. Slice the potatoes, aubergine and courgette. Cut cauliflower into florets. Deep fry all of them. Note: you can use only potatoes and aubergine if you like. Chop onion finely and fry in a little oil. Then take the fried potato and layer it over onions. Add the meat layer to cover the potatoes. Add another layer of potatoes. Add the layer of courgette and cauliflower. Then the aubergine layer. Finish with a layer of rice. Add 2 cups of the chicken stock and cook covered on very low heat until rice is cooked - about 45 minutes. Turn the heat off and leave to steam for at least 15 minutes. To serve – take a big round serving tray, cover the pan with it and carefully turn it upside down and slowly take pan away. Serve with salad or yoghurt.

Eman

Nyama muriwo with sadza

(Beef stew with maize)

Zimbabwean

Sadza is the staple food in Zimbabwe and is really satisfying with a thick tasty sauce.

Ingredients

For sadza
200g maize meal
1 L water
1 cup cold water

For stew
400g thinly sliced beef cut into 2" pieces
1 medium diced onion
1/2 tin of tomatoes
250g British spring greens
Crushed chilli to taste
Salt & pepper to taste

Method

For sadza Put maize meal into a pot and gradually add half a cup of water, mixing all the time to make a smooth paste. Place the pot on a medium hob. Gradually add 1 litre of boiling water to the maize paste and stir till mixture boils. Allow mixture to boil for 5 minutes and then remove the pot from the hob. Vary the consistency by increasing or decreasing the amount of maize meal. **For stew** Heat 2 spoons of oil in a pot and fry sliced beef. Add diced onion and 1/2 tin of tomatoes and mix. Add spring greens (shredded), a sprinkle of crushed chillies and salt and pepper to taste. Simmer for 10-15 minutes.

Schola

Penne paseana

Northern Italy Serves 4 people

Ingredients

500g penne pasta
1 green pepper
(cut into thin strips)
2 large onions, chopped
10 button mushrooms,
finely chopped
1 pinch of paprika
1 cup of pine nuts
Olive oil for frying

500g fresh chicken breast
fillets (cut into thin strips)
1 jar of pesto sauce (for ease...
make your own pesto if you wish)
2 cloves of garlic
1 pinch of cayenne pepper
Dried oregano (to taste)
Grated parmesan
Salt & pepper to taste

Method

Fill a large saucepan full of cold water. Add a glug of olive oil
and a pinch of sea salt. Once boiling, cook the penne pasta for
10-12 minutes. Whilst this is happening:
In a large frying pan, heat a generous glug of olive oil and lightly
fry the chicken breasts until starting to brown (ensure there is
no pink meat left). Add a large pinch of cayenne pepper,
paprika, and the garlic. Fry for a minute. Toss lightly and add the
onions. Once softened, add the green pepper. Once softened,
add the mushrooms and a generous dusting of oregano. After a
few minutes, add the pine nuts and fry on a high heat for about
2 minutes. Add the pesto. Season with salt and pepper. Once
pasta is cooked, drain and add to paesana sauce. Turn out into
a large serving dish and add copious shavings of parmesan.
Serve with some freshly baked ciabatta.

Mike

Pita od piletine (Chicken pie)

Serbian

Ingredients

1/4 small chicken cooked and broken into small bite sized
pieces (or you can use leftover cooked chicken).
2 tbsp vegetable oil
1 medium onion, finely chopped
3 tbsp sour cream

Batter mix

3 medium eggs
1 cup plain flour
1/2 tsp baking powder
1/2 L milk
1/2 tsp salt

Method for batter mix

Mix all the ingredients together to make a smooth batter, similar
to pancake mix.

Method for pie

Preheat the oven to Gas mark 6 (200°C/400°F). Add oil to deep
baking pot. Cover the bottom of the pot with chopped onion.
Sprinkle the chicken over onion. Add the batter mix. Bake in the
oven for 35 minutes. Once the pie is done cover it with sour
cream - evenly. Cut into square pieces. Serve with any salad.

Jelena

Pork belly

English Serves about 8

Ingredients for pork

The thick end of the belly
(last 6 ribs)

Fresh thyme leaves
Salt & fresh pepper

Ingredients for the apple sauce

3–4 large Bramley apples
1–2 tsp caster sugar (to taste)

A squeeze of lemon juice

Method for pork

Preheat the oven to Gas mark 7 (220°C/450°F). Score the skin of the belly with a sharp knife and rub with salt, pepper and fresh thyme leaves. Roast for 30 minutes, then turn the oven down to Gas mark 4 (180°C/350°F) and cook for roughly another hour, until the juices run clear when the meat is pierced with a skewer and the crackling has crackled to an irresistible golden brown. If the crackling is reluctant, whack up the heat again, as high as you like, and check every few minutes till it's done.

Method for the sauce

Peel, core and slice the Bramley apples, tossing them with he lemon juice as you go. Put them in a pan with a first sprinkling of sugar. Cook gently until the apples break up into a rough purée, then check for sweetness and adjust to your taste. Keep warm (or reheat gently to serve). Remove the crackling from the pork before carving, and then cut the joint into thick slices. Serve each person one or two slices with a good piece of crackling, and bring the apple sauce to the table. I like to serve this with mashed potatoes and lightly steamed greens.

Gavin

Pork belly with rice

Chinese Serves 4

Ingredients

12oz pork belly
12oz yellow split peas
12oz dry bamboo leaves
1 tbsp sugar
Light soya sauce to taste

1lb & 12oz glutinous rice
1/2 tsp five spice powder
1-2 tbsp light soy sauce
String for wrapping
Salt to taste

Method

Soak the glutinous rice and yellow split peas and bamboo leaves in separate bowls overnight. Next day, drain the water from the rice and peas and add sugar, salt and light soy sauce to each bowl and mix well.

Cut the pork belly into small square pieces and season with five spice powder, sugar, salt and light soy sauce.

Leave to marinate for 3 hours.

Drain the water from the bamboo.

Place two pieces of bamboo leaves over each other at right angles, cover with a layer of glutinous rice, then place a layer of split peas and add a piece of pork belly before adding another layer of rice.

Place two pieces of bamboo leaves at each side and wrap tightly, then tie up the rice package with a piece of string. Continue to make parcels until all the ingredients have been used. Boil the parcel's for 3 hours.

Jessica

V

Potato & cheese pierogi

Polish

Ingredients (potato and cheese filling)

1 tbsp grated onion
1 big onion chopped and fried
1 cup of cottage cheese
Salt & pepper

2 tbsp butter or oil
2 cups of cold
mashed potatoes

Method for filling

Fry the onion in a pan with oil until a nice gold/brown colour.
Combine it with cold potatoes and cheese. Season to taste with
salt and pepper. (Ingredients in the recipe can be in different
proportions depending on your taste.)

Ingredients (pierogi)

2 & 1/2 cups of flour
1 egg
3/4 cup warm water

1/2 tsp salt
2 tsp oil

Method for pierogi

Put flour into a deep bowl and add an egg, oil and water to
make a medium soft dough. Knead on a floured board until the
dough is smooth. Divide dough into two parts, cover and let it
stand for about 10 minutes. Prepare the filling and make sure
that it is thick enough to stay in the shape of a ball. Prepare
board for dough by putting a little amount of flour on it and roll
the dough quite thin. Cut rounds with the open end of a large
cup or a glass. (Continued on following page)

Put the round on your hand and put a spoon full of filling on it. Fold over the round to form half a circle.

Press the edges together with your fingers. Make sure that there is no filling on the edge and that everything sticks well together so the filling will not fall out during the boiling process. To be sure that pierogi are sealed well water the edges with a small amount of water. Place pierogi on a tea towel or clean cloth so it will keep its shape and cover it with another one to prevent them from drying. Boil a pot of water with a little bit of salt and then drop a few pierogi in it. Boil it like Tortellini. They will be ready when they are puffed up.

Don't forget to stir the water to separate pierogi from each other. When they are ready remove them into a colander and drain.

Pierogi should be served hot and fresh. For a better flavour they can be served with onions or sour cream.

Enjoy!

Joanna

Potato, bacon & onion surprise

English

Ingredients

1 packet of un-smoked bacon
4 large potatoes
Grated cheese

2 large onions
Extra virgin olive oil

Method

Pre-heat oven to Gas mark 6 (200°C/400°F), or moderately hot
Use a fair size baking dish and brush oil into the bottom
Place the peeled round sliced potatoes into the dish and
sprinkle on a little oil.
Then layer with onions, sprinkle of oil and then bacon.
Repeat layering until you end with potatoes as the last layer.
Place in the oven for 45 minutes and cook until golden on top.
Garnish with grated cheese and herbs and serve with
watercress green salad

Margaret

V

Rice with garlic

Brazilian Serves 3 people

Since I was a child in Brazil I used to eat rice every day for my lunch and dinner together with chicken or with famous Brazilian soft meats.
I learnt to prepare this recipe in Brazil before coming to England as a volunteer. Although the first attempt was quite bad, now I can do it very easily and everybody enjoys it.

Ingredients

1/2 cup of olive oil
1/2 mug of long grain rice
2 cups boiled water
1 tsp salt

1/2 onion sliced
1 clove of garlic,
sliced very thinly

Method

Put olive oil in a pan and sauté onion and garlic in the oil on a low heat until garlic is crispy and light golden brown.
After that sauté the rice for about 3 minutes and add water and salt. Wait for 30 minutes and it is done.
Options: Serve with vegetables and fish or any kind of meat.
Enjoy!

Russian borscht

Russian

Ingredients

Any type of meat
2 heads of uncooked beetroot
1 tin of plum tomatoes
1 green pepper chopped
1 L water

1 medium cabbage
3 carrots
2-3 bay leaves
1-2 chopped onions
Salt & pepper to taste

Method

Tenderise the meat and cut in into small pieces. Add in pot with water. Cook it for two hours to get a meat stock in water. When it is cooked add 1-2 chopped onions.
After 10 minutes add uncooked and grated beetroot, finely grated cabbage, grated carrots, chopped plum tomatoes and green pepper. Add the bay leaves, salt and pepper.
Cook for 20-25 minutes until vegetables are tender. Serve with sour cream or mayonnaise. Add coriander or dill if you like.

Tamila

V

Sabzi polo Persian rice

Persian Serves 6

Ingredients

5 small cups of basmati rice
125ml olive oil
1 fish stock cube
(omit to keep it vegetarian)
1 tsp cayenne pepper
10 spring onions, green ends only
150ml sabzi polo (Asian shops),
if you cannot get it, use more dill weed
2.5cm ginger, grated
75g dry onion

7 small cups of water
1 heaped tsp turmeric
2 vegetable stock cubes
1 whole garlic bulb,
crushed
159ml dill weed
2 cups peas
2 cups sweetcorn
15 strands saffron

Method

Add the rice to a large non stick saucepan. Add water and olive oil. Add turmeric. Put the stock cubes in a bowl and dissolve in a little water. Add the dissolved cubes to the saucepan and add saffron. Bring to the boil. Add cayenne, pepper, dill weed and sabzi polo. Add peas and sweetcorn, ginger, garlic and dried onions. Stir gently. Add chopped spring onions and then drizzle a little olive oil over the top of the mixture. Cover saucepan and continue boiling on semi hot heat for 15 minutes. Lower heat and cook for further 45 minutes.

Dill weed is the bright green leaves of the dill plant with a subtle, delicate flavour.

Parvaneh

Sajur lodeh (Vegetables in coconut milk)
Indonesian

Almost any green vegetables, red or green peppers and aubergine can be used. It is not advised that root vegetables are used however. All the vegetables are cooked together, however add those that need longer cooking first, leaving the fastest to cook last.

Vegetable ingredients
Good handful of green beans
Small green or white cabbage cut into strips
1 courgette cut into inch pieces
Small aubergine cut into inch cubes

Ingredients:
1 onion
1 red chilli
1/2 sereh (lemon grass)
cut lengthways
1 tsp ground cumin
1 tin coconut milk (use a good quality that has plenty of thick coconut milk)
Assam (tamarind water) – use about a teaspoon of tamarind paste or a walnut sized piece of dried tamarind in half cup of hot water. (Continued on following page)

1 clove garlic
1/2 inch piece of laos (galangal)
Salaam leaf (if available)
2 heaped tsp ground coriander seed
Trasi – small amount (dash of Thai fish sauce as an alternative)
Vegetables – see above
Brown sugar to taste
Salt to taste

Method

Mince onion, garlic and chilli in a pestle and mortar or electric blender until it is a rough paste (not too smooth).

Fry paste mixture for a few minutes until it becomes cooked. Add coriander and cumin and stir in for a few seconds then slowly add the coconut milk stirring continuously.

Add the other spices, tamarind and sugar and then add the vegetables, first adding the green beans. After 2-3 minutes add the cabbage. Cook for about 5 minutes then add the courgette and aubergine. More water may be required – if you add water, fast boil with the lid off to reduce the sauce.

Cook for another 5-6 minutes. The vegetables need to be cooked but still firm. The end result should be a mixture of vegetables coated in a rich coconut sauce.

Remember to remove the lemon grass and galangal as this is for flavouring only.

Really good on its own with plain boiled rice and a hot chilli relish or served as an accompaniment to a meat dish.

Note: Indonesian meat curries might use the same ingredients and broadly the same process as above substituting the vegetables for meat (lamb or chicken) and frying the meat before adding the coconut milk but could also include a wider range of dried spices such as cloves, cinnamon and fennel seeds.

Mike

Seafood rice

Portuguese Serves 4

Ingredients
3 medium onions – thickly sliced
2 green peppers – thickly sliced
3 ripe tomatoes - thickly sliced
Olive oil
Salt & pepper
Paprika
Seafood cocktail
250g easy cook rice
Fresh coriander
Optional – chilli powder

Method
Coat a heavy based pan in olive oil.
Add onions, green peppers and tomatoes.
Fry together for 2 minutes.
Add seafood mix and fry for 15–20 minutes.
Add chopped coriander.
Add rice.
Reduce heat and steam until
rice cooked.
(add water if dry).

Theresa

Somali crabmeat stew

Somali

Ingredients
480ml white rice
960ml water
60ml peanut oil or butter
240ml onions, finely chopped
1 tsp curry powder
1 tsp powdered ginger
1 tsp salt
1 tsp crushed red pepper flakes
1 tbsp tomatoes cut in small wedges
908g crab meat or other seafood such as scallops

Optional: empty scallop shells for serving

Method
In a saucepan, wash and rinse the rice.
Add the water, cover and bring to the boil.
Reduce heat and let simmer for 15-20 minutes.
Meanwhile, heat the oil or butter in a deep, heavy saucepan.
Add the onions, curry, ginger, salt and red pepper flakes, and sauté until the onions are lightly browned.
Add the tomatoes and simmer until soft.
Add the crabmeat or other seafood and sauté for 10 minutes.
Serve over the rice in scooped-out scallops shells or alone.

Abdullahi

97

Stewed guinea fowl with nuts

Zambian

Ingredients
1 guinea fowl cut into pieces
1 large onion, sliced or chopped
3/4 cup cooked & sifted ground nuts or peanut butter
Enough water to cover the guinea fowl
Salt to taste
Cayenne/chilli powder optional

Method
Boil fowl with onions until tender, making sure there is enough water to make the sauce. When fowl is ready, make a paste with water and sifted ground nuts or peanut butter and add to the pot. Add salt to taste. Boil for 20 minutes until the nuts are cooked and sauce is thick enough. Cayenne pepper or chilli can be added if preferred.
You can substitute the guinea fowl with chicken cooked in water for 30-45 minutes.

This is a Zambian dish and is served with Maize meal (See Sadza, recipe on page 83).

Norah

V

Swabian käsespätzle

German Serves 4 people

Ingredients

500g flour
1 tsp salt for spaetzle
At least 500g Emmentale
cheese (or any other cheese
that melts well)
Salt & pepper to taste

4 eggs
Nutmeg
4 medium to large onions
Butter or oil for frying
1 cup water

Method

Heat oil in a small pot and put sliced or chopped onions in it.
Sauté onions. **Spaetzle:** Mix flour and salt together. Break the
eggs into the flour and stir well. Add a little nutmeg. Pour in
water and stir again. The dough should not become too
smooth. Bring slightly salted water to a boil and add a little oil
to prevent the spaetzle from sticking. If you have a spaetzle mill
follow the instructions if not, press the dough through the holes
of a large colander into the boiling water. Don't forget to stir or
the spaetzle will stick together.
Boil until the spaetzle are al dente. Drain the spaetzle in a
colander. Now begin quickly to layer spaetzle, grated cheese,
salt and pepper in this order into a bowl or pot. The cheese
melts best when spaetzle are still hot. Wait one minute after
you have finished the layering and then take two spoons and
mix the kaesespaetzle in the bowl or pot again. Serve on a plate
and put the onions on top. Add more salt and pepper if you like.

Carolyn

Toad in the hole

English

This is an old, post war family recipe.

Ingredients

4oz self raising flour
1 egg
1 level tbsp butter, melted
1/2 finely chopped onion

Pinch of salt
1/2 pint milk
1 lb sausages, any type
Olive oil

Method

Preheat the oven to Gas mark 7 (220°C/450°F). Sift flour and salt into a bowl.
Add the egg, milk and melted butter.
Beat to a batter - until it clings to a fork and does not run off.
Stir in chopped onion. Cover the bottom of a deep baking tray with olive oil and warm it up in the oven. Add the sausages, and bake them for 7 minutes if they are very thick. No need for the baking if you are using thin sausages. Pour the batter over sausages and bake for 30 minutes on Gas mark 6 (200°C/400°F). After 30 minutes test if it is done: pierce the batter with the fork. If the batter sticks to the fork, bake for another 15 minutes.

Lynda

V
Toor dahl

Indian Cooking time 20 minutes in pressure cooker

Ingredients

1 cup toor dahl
1 tsp haldi/turmeric
1 tsp chopped coriander (fresh leaves)
Salt to taste
Pinch of sugar
2 cloves
Pinch of hing/asafoetida powder
1/2 tsp lemon juice
2-3 cups water

1 tin chopped tomatoes
Green chillies to taste
1/2 tsp garam masala
1/2 tsp mustard seeds
1/2 tsp chopped ginger
1 cinnamon stick
Curry leaves
Oil for frying seeds

Method

Wash the dahl in warm water 3 times. Then boil in a
pressure cooker until it whistles 3-5 times. Once tender, use a
blender and mix up into a soup-like consistency (no lumps). In a
separate pan, heat the oil and add the cumin, mustard and curry
leaves and cover. Once they have started 'popping', add the
hing and cover again. Then add the tomatoes and fresh chillies.
Leave uncovered for a few minutes. Add the salt, turmeric,
lemon juice, sugar and ginger. Stir and leave for 2-3 minutes on
a high heat. Once the tomatoes are tender and have turned to
puree, add the blended toor dahl to it with a little boiling water.
Bring to the boil and then simmer on a low heat for 10-15
minutes. Take off the heat and add the coriander leaves and
garam masala. Keep covered until you are ready to serve.

Suhana Group

Beef & fresh vegetable salad

Russian

Ingredients

Equal quantities of:

Carrots	Beetroot
Spring onion	Potatoes
Fresh white cabbage	Salt and pepper to taste
Mayonnaise	Oil for frying
Beef	

Method

Grate carrots and beetroot and finely chop spring onions and cabbage.

Cut potato into chips shaped pieces and boil.

Cut beef into fine strips, add to a small amount of boiling water, and cook until done.

Remove from water and fry for a very short time.

Mix all the ingredients together, add mayonnaise, and salt and pepper to taste.

Tany

V
Beetroot salad

Azerbaijani

Ingredients
500g grated cooked beetroot
1-2 crushed garlic cloves
50g crushed walnuts
Salt
4-5 tsp of mayonnaise

Method
Mix all together

Tamila

Chilli oil

Portuguese

Ingredients
1/2 kg bag whole dry red chillies
Brandy
Vegetable oil

Method
Fill a big jar up with chillies
Add 1 measure of brandy and shake until all the brandy is
absorbed.
Open the jar and fill it up with vegetable oil.

Use it in salad dressings, or in seafood recipes.

Theresa

V

Fig chutney

English
Makes about 2 kg (4lb)

Ingredients
1.25 L (2 pints) red wine vinegar
500g (1lb) light soft brown sugar
2 tbsp sea salt
1kg (2lb) slightly under ripe black figs (the ones from South West France are ideal)
500g (1lb) onions
250g (8oz) pitted dates
150g (5oz) fresh ginger root
2 tbsp sweet paprika
1 tbsp white mustard seeds
1 tbsp dried tarragon

Method
Put the vinegar, sugar, and salt into a large pan, stirring until the sugar and salt have dissolved.
Bring to the boil, then simmer for about 5 minutes.
Slice figs and onions: coarsely chop dates: finely shred ginger root. Add to the pan with paprika and mustard seeds, bring to the boil, then simmer for 1 hour. Remove from the heat, add the tarragon; mix well. Ladle into hot sterilized jars; seal.

The chutney will be ready in 1 month. It goes really well with cheddar cheese for a 'ploughman's' lunch.

Paula

V

Gaddo gaddo sauce
(Peanut sauce)
Indonesian Serves 4

Ingredients

1 onion
1 red chilli
1/2 sereh (lemon grass) cut lengthways
3 dsp of crunchy peanut butter
Brown sugar to taste
Salt & pepper to taste

1 clove garlic
1/2 inch piece of laos (galangal)
1 tin coconut milk
Assam (tamarind water) – use about 1 tsp of tamarind paste or a walnut sized piece of dried tamarind in half cup of hot water.

Note – there is one other ingredient, salaam leaf which is difficult to find in the UK. If you can get it use one or two. There is no substitute.

Method

Mince onion, garlic and chilli in a pestle and mortar or electric blender until it is a rough paste (not too smooth).
Fry paste mixture for a few minutes until it becomes cooked.
Slowly add the coconut milk stirring continuously.
Add the other spices tamarind and sugar and simmer for about 15 minutes to let the spices blend. Finally add the peanut butter and stir well until thoroughly mixed. Add salt to taste.The dish is finished. It can be quite thick or thinner according to preference and easily adjusted by just adding a little water.

Mike

V

Ginger chutney

Indian

Ingredients

1/4 cup ginger, pealed
1 tomato, pealed
1 tsp fresh mint
2-3 spring onions
Salt to taste

1 green mango, pealed
1 tsp coriander leaves
1-4 green chillies, depending
on taste

Method

Chop all the ingredients and then mash together

Suhana Group

V

Green chilli salad

Afghani

Ingredients
Iceberg lettuce, chopped
5 green chillies
Bunch fresh coriander, chopped
Handful fresh mint leaves, chopped
Cucumber, diced
3 tomatoes, diced
Salt to taste

Method
Roughly chop the iceberg lettuce.
Add 1 deseeded and chopped green chilli.
Add chopped coriander and mint.
Mix together (use your hands).
Rinse thoroughly under a running cold tap.
Drain and place in salad bowl.
Add another chopped chilli.
Add diced cucumber.
Add diced tomatoes.

Mix together and add 3 whole chillies
to garnish.
Add salt to taste.

Samya

V

Mixed bean salad

Greek

Ingredients
2 cups mixed dry beans; butter, haricot & sugar beans
1 large onion
1/4 cup oil (olive)
Salt to taste
Enough water to cover beans

Method
Soak the beans 4-5 hours in advance.
Cook beans in water till soft.
Add onion and when it is cooked add oil and salt.
Allow to boil for another 30-60 minutes, making sure that there is enough water to cook the beans.
Once cooked, serve with a salad made with onion, tomato and olive oil and eat with fresh bread.

Beans are a Greek staple food. My late father came from Myteleni Island in Greece and this one of the many lovely recipes.

Norah

V

Raitha

Indian

Ingredients

500g natural yogurt
Salt to taste
Ground black pepper
Coriander for garnish

1/2 cup of milk
2 handfuls of boondi - you
can buy ready made in Asian
Food stores, or make your own

Method

Mix yogurt with a little milk.
Add salt to taste.
Add boondi (2 handfuls).
Sprinkle pinch of black pepper.
Leave in fridge until ready to serve.
Sprinkle with a little coriander before serving.

Ingredients to make your own Boondi

2 cups yoghurt
1/2 tsp cumin powder
Red chilli powder to taste
Finely chopped coriander leaves

100g gram flour
Salt to taste
1/4 tsp garam masala
Oil for frying

Method for boondi

Add water to gram flour and mix well to form a paste.
Add salt other spices and mix some more. Heat oil.
Pass the paste through a draining spoon (you get little dough
droplets) and fry till golden.

Veena

V

Russian red bean salad

Russian

Ingredients
1 can of plain red kidney beans
3-4 gherkins, diced
1 onion, diced
Chopped parsley
2 tbsp of vegetable oil
Mayonnaise
1 clove of garlic
Handful of breadcrumbs

Method
Shallow fry diced onion in 2 table spoons of vegetable oil.
Add the chopped parsley, bread crumbs and crushed garlic.
Drain kidney beans and add with gherkins. Mix well.
Add mayonnaise, salt and pepper to taste.

Tany

V

Red pepper chutney

Indian

Ingredients
3 red peppers
1 tsp red chilli powder
Pinch of salt
Pinch of sugar/sweetener
1 fresh lemon, use all the flesh and juice
2 fresh tomatoes

Method
Chop all ingredients and put in liquidiser to puree.

Suhana Group

Tuna salad (Low fat)

Persian Serves 6
This is a healthy alternative to tuna and mayonnaise salad.

Ingredients
3 tins tuna   10 whites of spring onion

For seasoning
Olive oil   Cayenne Pepper
Turmeric   Squeeze lemon
Squeeze lime   Red chillies for garnish

Method
Drain tins of tuna and place in a mixing bowl.
Add chopped spring onions.
And seasoning to taste.
Garnish with red chillies.

Parvaneh

Warm potato and sausage salad

English

Ingredients

1lb Maris Piper or Edwards potatoes
1 large smoked sausage or 8 Frankfurters (ready cooked)
1 large onion
4-5 gherkins (optional)
Mayonnaise and salad cream to taste (half and half)

Method

Peel potatoes and cut into smallish chunks and boil till fairly soft. Finely chop onion, gherkins and sausage, put into a mixing bowl. Add in hot potatoes along with mayo and salad cream and mix all the ingredients together. Serve while still hot or can be eaten cold.

Bev

V

Yogurt chutney

Indian

Ingredients
Cup of plain yogurt
1 tsp salt
1 tsp coriander
Finely chopped green chilli
1 tsp mint sauce

Method
Add in seasoning and spices to yogurt and mix well.

Gurbax

V

Apple crumble

English

Ingredients

8oz plain flour
4oz butter/margarine
1 flat tsp cinnamon
1 tsp ground nutmeg
2 tbsp water

8oz caster/granulated sugar
4 large Bramley (or similar)
apples peeled & sliced
1 pinch of salt

Method

Pre-heat the oven to Gas mark 6 (400°F/200°C).
Rub the butter/margarine into the flour.
Mix in half of the sugar, half of the spices, and a pinch of salt.
Place the sliced apple in an open oven proof dish and stir in the
remaining half of the sugar, spices and water.
Pour the crumble mixture over the top.
Bake for 45 minutes.
Serve with custard, ice-cream or yoghurt.

Lynda

V

Baklava

Turkish

Ingredients

Syrup
1 & 1/2 cups water
2 cups sugar
1 tbsp lemon juice
5 tbsp whipping cream

Baklava
300g filo pastry (18-20 sheets)
1 cup unsalted melted butter
1 cup pistachios, roughly ground

Method

Syrup
To prepare the baklava syrup place the water and sugar in a pot. First bring to a boil and continue boiling for 5 minutes. Then simmer for 15 minutes and turn the heat off. Add lemon juice.

Base
Preheat the oven to Gas mark 5 (375°F/190°C). Place the block of filo sheets on the counter. Cut the sheets in half. Now there are two blocks of approximately 40 sheets. After cutting in half, the size of the sheets should be the same as the size of the oven dish. Keep the blocks separate as half the sheets will go below the baklava filling, and the rest above. Brush the inside of the oven dish with the butter. Then lay down 2 sheets. Spread more butter on top, and then place two more sheets on top and butter again. Continue until you finish the first block of the filo sheets. Then spread the cream evenly on top. Spread the pistachios on the cream evenly. Then finish second block of the sheets the same way. Don't forget to brush the very top with

butter. Dip a big, sharp knife into hot water to cut the baklava in rectangles.

Cut 4 vertically and 5 horizontally to get 20 pieces.

However, don't cut all the way down, only cut halfway until you reach the pistachios. This will ensure only the top part will rise when you bake it. Place the dish on the middle rack. Bake for 25 minutes. At this point turn the heat down to Gas mark 3 (325°F/165°C) while the dish is still in the oven. Bake for 30 more minutes and take the baklava out. Leave it at room temperature for 10 minutes.

Then re-cut the baklava all the way down. This part may be a little bit hard.

With a tablespoon pour the lukewarm syrup evenly along the cut lines. Make sure not to pour it all over, only between the lines. Sprinkle some pistachios on top.

Let it rest at least 4 hours before serving. The syrup should be completely absorbed.

You don't need to refrigerate it. Cover it loosely with foil.

V

Banana breakfast pancakes

English Makes 5-6 pancakes

Ingredients
1 large or two small Fairtrade ripe bananas (the riper the better)
100g (4oz) self-raising flour
Fair-trade Demerara sugar to taste
1 organic egg
A pinch of salt
A pinch of grated cinnamon and or nutmeg (optional)
1 knob of butter (optional)
Milk to mix
Chocolate chips (optional)

Method
Peel and mash bananas. In a large bowl put all ingredients together and mix well with enough milk to make a thick batter. Leave to stand for about 10 minutes. Heat a large frying pan or similar utensil. Brush on a little fat – oil or butter. Pour a ladle full of pancake mixture on to the greased pan and spread evenly to form a circle about 14cm (6 inches) in diameter. Using a spatula or similar instrument gently lift off base and turn once or twice. Remove from pan and continue the same process until all the batter is used. Each pancake should take about one minute to cook. Add a handful of chocolate chips to the batter for a banana/chocolate chip pancake. Serve hot or cold on it's own or with butter and/or syrup.

Amna

V

Banana cake

English 18 portions

Ingredients

650g bananas (skin on)
450g granulated sugar
30g baking powder
2 eggs
120ml milk

220g margarine
540g flour
1 level tsp Bicarbonate
of soda

Method

Preheat the oven to Gas mark 4 (180°C/350°F).
Cream the margarine and sugar until soft.
Peel and break up the bananas.
Add the bananas and other ingredients to creamed margarine.
Beat well. Put mix into a well greased and floured tin.
Bake for 1 hour.
Remove from oven and leave for one day before turning out.

Martin

V

Bread & butter pudding

English

Ingredients
3 slices of white bread & butter
2-3oz dried fruit
1 - 1 & 1/2oz caster sugar
2 eggs
3/4 pint whole fat milk (warm)
Brown sugar
Cinnamon

Method
Preheat the oven to Gas mark 3-4 (160-180°C/325-350°F).
Cut bread and butter into triangles, put in an oven proof dish and add fruit.
Beat eggs with caster sugar and pour in warm milk then strain over the bread.
Sprinkle with brown sugar and cinnamon.
Place in the oven until just firm and set, approximately 45 minutes.

You could make this recipe healthier by using brown bread and skimmed milk.

Sandra

V

Auntie Dort's caramel slice

Australian

Ingredients
1 cup soft brown sugar
4oz butter
1 beaten egg
1 cup chopped dates or sultanas
1 cup self raising flour

Method
Pre-heat oven to Gas mark 4/5 (350-375°F/180-190°C).
Melt butter and sugar in pan.
Add well beaten egg to dry ingredients with melted butter and sugar.
Pour into greased slab tin and bake for 20 minutes.

Pat

V

Chocolate pot heaven

English

A very simple chocolate dessert especially if you have an electric blender.

Ingredients

200g plain or dark chocolate   300ml single cream
3-4 drops of extract of vanilla essence   1 egg

Method

If using a blender, break the chocolate into small pieces into the blender container. Scald the cream in a small saucepan or in a non-metallic bowl in the microwave until just boiling. Then pour immediately onto the chocolate in the blender and blend until smooth. Finally add the vanilla and the whole egg. Blend again until smooth. If you do not have a blender, scald the cream, take it off the heat and add the chocolate. Leave for a few minutes for the chocolate to melt, then stir until smooth. Finally add the vanilla and egg. Beat over a low heat until absolutely smooth. Pour into 4-6 individual pots or ramekin dishes and chill for about 3 hours before serving. The mixture will set to a thick, smooth and delicious chocolate cream.

Serve either unadorned or with chocolate curls shaved off a chocolate bar with a potato peeler and little macaroon biscuits.

Sally

V

Chocolate sponge cake

English

Ingredients
Sponge

8oz self raising flour (sifted)
8oz caster sugar
2 large eggs

2 tsp baking powder
2oz cocoa powder
8oz butter

Butter cream filling & icing

3oz margarine

6oz icing sugar

Method
Sponge

Pre-heat the oven to Gas mark 4 (350F/180°C). Cream together the butter and the sugar. Beat the eggs and then gradually add to the butter and sugar mixture stirring continuously until smooth. Next add the flour and baking powder gradually, stirring continuously until smooth. Pour into two 8 inch cake tins and bake in the oven for 45 minutes. Once cooked remove from oven, allow to cool then remove from tins.

Butter cream icing for the filling

Mix the margarine and icing sugar together until smooth (adding more icing sugar if needed).

Once the cakes are cool spread one of them with half of the butter cream mixture and place the other cake on top. Spread the remaining butter cream mixture on top.

Jackie

V

Quick cake

Serbian

Ingredients

1 box sweet sponge fingers
1 L milk (for cream)
1 egg
2 bags vanilla sugar
(available at Polish shops)
2 tbsp sugar to sprinkle
over strawberries

2 bags vanilla cream
2 packs 'dream topping' cream
Milk for dream topping cream
1-2 cups of strawberries
Sliver of unsalted butter
Handful ground walnuts
(optional)

Method

In a deep square, mould layer the biscuits. Add 1 bag of
vanilla sugar to milk for the vanilla blancmange cream and cook
according to the instructions on the bag. Beat an egg and add
to the vanilla cream. Remove from heat and add butter.
Pour over biscuits immediately. Sprinkle sugar over
strawberries.
Cover the biscuits and cream base with strawberries and leave
it to cool. Make Dream Topping cream according to the
instructions on the package. Add the remaining bag of vanilla
sugar to the Dream Topping. Cover the strawberries with the
Dream Topping. Keep in the fridge to set. Sprinkle with ground
walnuts (optional).

Drazena

Fairtrade mincemeat

English

Ingredients

500g Fairtrade raisins
500g Fairtrade mixed fruit
500g suet
Rind of 1 lemon & 1 orange
Juice of half lemon & half orange
1/2 pint of Fairtrade rum

500g Fairtrade sultanas
1 kg apples – peeled
850g Fairtrade brown
caster sugar
1 tsp ground cinnamon

Method

Mince all dried fruit and apples.
Add all other ingredients.
Mix well and leave in covered bowl.
Stir every day for 1 week.
Put into jars leaving a space at the top.
Cover and keep for several weeks for the best results.
This makes about 8lbs of delicious mincemeat.

Anne

V

Fyrste kake (Almond cake)

Norwegian

Ingredients

2 egg yolks
6oz sugar
1 tbsp baking powder
6oz ground almonds
4 egg whites

3 tsp double cream
13oz self-rising flour
8oz margarine
9oz icing sugar

Method

Preheat the oven to Gas mark 4 (180°C/350°F).
Whip egg yolks, cream and sugar together for a good 5 minutes
– until the mixture becomes very thick. Sieve in the flour and
baking powder. Mix in the margarine. Roll out the pastry and
line the tin with 2/3 of pastry. Beat the egg whites until very
stiff. Grind the almonds, sieve icing sugar over and fold in the
beaten egg whites. Place on top of the pastry. Lattice with
remaining pastry and bake for 30 minutes.

Kirsten

V

Golden apple tart

English

Ingredients
1/2lb short crust pastry
1 medium apple
3 tbsp golden syrup
3 tbsp fine breadcrumbs
1 tsp sugar

Method
Pre-heat the oven to Gas mark 6 (400°F/200°C).
Line an 8" tin with thin pastry.
Peel and core the apple and cut into sections and line evenly on pastry. Warm the syrup and spread evenly over the apples.
Top with the bread crumbs and sprinkle sugar on top.
Bake for 15 minutes or until golden.

Jean

V

Hurry up apple cake

English

This was one of my mum's favourite recipes. I hope you enjoy it as much as she did!

Ingredients

4oz soft margarine or butter
2 large eggs
1/4 tsp vanilla essence
2oz chopped prunes (optional)

3oz caster sugar
4oz self raising flour, sifted
with 1 level tsp baking powder

Topping:
1oz butter or margarine (to grease baking tin)
2oz soft brown sugar
1 large cooking apple (peeled & cored) – I use more apples
7 prunes (optional)

Method

Set oven to moderate Gas mark 4 (175°C/325°F). Spread the 1oz of butter over base of tin then sprinkle brown sugar evenly over it. Slice apple into 7 rings and place in a slightly overlapping circle on top of the sugar. Place a prune in the centre of each apple slice.

Assembling the cake

Place all the ingredients in a large bowl and beat with a wooden spoon for 3–4 minutes until well mixed. Alternatively use an electric mixer for 1–2 minutes. Spoon the cake mixture over the apples, levelling the top with the back of a spoon. Bake just above the centre of the oven for 40 minutes. Serve as a cake or warm as a pudding with custard or cream.

Marion

V

Kaffee klatsch kuchen

German

Ingredients

3.5 oz (100g) butter or margarine
1 packet vanilla sugar
Pinch of salt
1oz (30g) corn flour
0.75 oz (20g) plain chocolate, grated
Icing sugar for dusting

2.5oz (70g) sugar
1 egg
3.5oz (100g) self raising flour
1.5oz (45g) ground almonds
0.5oz (15g) mixed dried fruit
A little milk

Method

Pre-heat oven to Gas mark 3 (325°F/170°C)
Cream the fat and gradually add the sugar, vanilla sugar, egg and salt. Mix and sieve together the flour and corn flour and add to the creamed mixture, one tablespoon at a time. Fold in each tablespoon before adding the next.
Carefully fold in the almonds, chocolate and mixed dried fruit
Add a little milk until the mixture gets to a heavy dropping consistency. Grease a small (1lb) loaf tin and line with greaseproof paper and fill with the cake mixture.
Bake for about 45 minutes.
Remove from oven and leave to cool.
Remove from tin and dust with icing sugar.

V

Lemon babka cake

Polish

Lemon babka cake has traditionally been baked by my mother Gabriela for Easter. There are many varieties of babka, including babka made of yeast dough; though in my humble opinion, the lemon babka is the best.

Ingredients
For cake
5 eggs (weigh them together their shells and make a note of total weight)
1 heaped tsp baking powder
Juice & grated peel of 1 lemon
Some breadcrumbs

Equal amounts of:
(each ingredient the same weight as the total weight of the eggs) sugar, butter & plain flour
Butter to grease the mould/tin

For lemon icing
1 egg yolk
Icing sugar

Juice of 1 lemon

Method
For the cake
Pre-heat oven Gas mark 4-5 (350-375°F/180-190°C).
Whisk the eggs & sugar in a mixer/blender.
Add baking powder, flour, lemon juice and grated lemon peel.
Melt the butter and pour it into the mixture, mixing all the time
Pour the mixture into a mould or tin, previously buttered and sprinkled with breadcrumbs. (Continued on following page)

Put in a pre-heated oven and bake for 50 minutes (keep an eye on the cake whilst cooking to ensure it doesn't burn)
Remove from oven, cool and then remove from mould/tin

Lemon icing
Whisk the yolk of 1 egg.
Add the lemon juice and icing sugar. Keep adding icing sugar until mixture thickens.
Spread the icing on the cooled cake.

It's best to leave the cake overnight to allow the icing to dry.

Gabriela

V

Lemon drizzle cake

English

Ingredients

2 eggs
6oz self raising flour
6oz caster sugar
Finely grated rind of 1 lemon

4oz soft margarine
1 tsp baking powder
4 tbsp milk

Topping
Juice of 1 lemon
4 oz granulated sugar

Method

Heat oven to Gas mark 4 (180°C/350F°).
Grease and line 2 x 1 lb loaf tins.
Mix all ingredients in large bowl and beat well for 2 minutes.
Divide between 2 tins and level surface.
Bake for 30-40 minutes until cooked and springs back.

Topping
Whilst baking make topping.
Place lemon juice and sugar in small bowl and stir to mix.
When loaves are cooked spread lemon mixture over baked loaves while still warm and leave to cool.

V

Marmalade

English

Ingredients

1lb / 2 large grapefruits
1lb oranges
3 pints sugar
2 & 1/2 pints water for fruit

2 lemons
3 pints water
3 cinnamon sticks
1/2 pint water for pips and pith

Method

Wash and shred the fruit. Remove the thick pith and pips and keep. Put the fruit and the peel into water and leave it overnight to soak. Put the pips and the pith in a basin with water and leave over night
Strain the pith and pips, keeping the water.
Add the water in which the pips and the pith were soaked to the fruit and peel. Bring to the boil
Simmer for 1 & 1/2 hours – until fruit is soft.
Add sugar and bring to the boil. Boil rapidly until setting point is reached, which is approximately 15-20 minutes. When the high frothing stops and boiling becomes noisy, giving a 'plop' sound, you will know that you have reached the setting point.
Once cooled, put in clear jars.

Use within 2 weeks, as there are no preservatives in this marmalade.

Lynda

Nan Coopers Christmas pudding

English

Nan gave a hand written copy of this recipe to my mum sometime in the 1970's and mum has used it ever since. Nobody is sure how old the recipe is, but it at least dates back to Nan's grandmother. I suppose technically it's more of a template than a recipe.

Ingredients

3/4lb raisins
1lb currants
1 pack shredded suet
1/2 lb soft brown sugar
1 large loaf white bread crumbled
Juice & grated peel of 1 orange
1/2 tsp freshly grated nutmeg
4 large eggs
1 pint milk

3/4lb sultanas
1/2lb mixed peel
1/2lb plain flour
2 finely grated carrots
Juice & grated peel of 1 lemon
2 tsp mixed spice
Pinch of salt
1 bottle of Barley wine

Method

Mix dry ingredients well in a large bowl. You can do this with a wooden spoon. I prefer to use my (clean) hands and get messy- it also seems to mix better then. Work the eggs into the mixture and then gradually do the same with the barley wine and milk, so that the dry ingredients begin to absorb the liquids. For this I do use a wooden spoon. (Continued on following page)

Cover and leave to stand overnight. The next step is a very important part of our Christmas tradition! The mixture should have soaked up a large proportion of the liquid, but should still be moist and be quite hard work to stir. If it's dry, add some more alcohol or milk. Everyone in the family must take it in turns to stir the mixture 3 times. As the spoon goes round the mixture for the third time, you should make a wish. You must complete this by the end of the third stir, or it won't come true! Spoon the mixture into well-greased pudding bowls that are suitable for boiling. Place a circle of greased, grease-proof paper (to stop the mixture sticking to the lid) on top of the mixture, before you place the lid on. Place each bowl in a saucepan with boiling water deep enough to come between 1/2 and 3/4 of the way up the bowl and boil gently for about 8 hours (for a 2 pint pudding bowl). Make sure that you regularly top up the water. Traditionally the grease-proof paper was topped with muslin and tied, but the lid to the bowl works just as well, if not better. Allow to cool. The puddings can then be stored in a dry cupboard for at least 6 months.
We normally make them between July and September.
On Christmas day, boil a 2lb pudding for about 3 hours, and then serve. Traditionally the pudding is served flaming! Just heat some Brandy, pour over the pudding and then set light to the Brandy. The brandy tends to be much easier to light if you warm it first. The pudding is traditionally served with brandy sauce, but can be served with custard or cream.

The puddings mature in storage and seem to taste better, the longer they are kept.

Nan Cooper

V

Napoleon cake

Azerbaijani

Ingredients
1 (1/2kg) packet of puff pastry
600ml fresh double cream
200g sugar
1 packet of vanilla sugar (available in Polish shops)

Method
Cut pastry into 4 pieces and roll each piece to be 2mm thick.
Bake each piece for 5 minutes, or until they get golden colour.
Cut off the pastry edges, but keep the off-cuts.
Mix cream, sugar and vanilla sugar together.
Place one sheet of baked pastry on a serving tray, cover with cream, and repeat until all the pastry sheets are used.
Cover the top layer with the cream.
Grind the pastry off-cuts with the rolling pin and sprinkle over the cream.
Leave it in a fridge to set.
Cut into square pieces and serve.

Tamila

V

Pancake bake

French

Ingredients

250g / 9 oz flour
4 eggs
100g / 4oz prunes

150g / 5 oz sugar
1 L milk
Rum

Method

Pre-heat the oven to Gas mark 6(400°F/200C).
Remove the stones from the prunes.
Place the prunes in a shallow dish and cover with rum, leave to soak. Mix together the flour, sugar and eggs.
Pour the milk in gradually, still mixing as you go until the mixture is smooth. Add the prunes and rum.
Pour into an oven proof dish.
Bake for about 45 minutes until the mixture is set.

Daniel
www.recipe-ideas.org

V

Pineapple cake

English

Ingredients

1 cup of sugar
4oz butter
1 cup of plain flour
1lb mixed dried fruit
1 tsp bicarbonate of soda

13oz / 1 tin crushed pineapple
1 cup of self raising flour
2 eggs (size 3)
1 tsp mixed spice

Method

Pre-heat oven to Gas mark 3 (325°F/160-170°C). Put sugar, butter, mixed fruit, drained pineapple, mixed spice and baking soda in a saucepan. Boil for 3 minutes. Remove pan from heat and allow mixture to cool. Once mixture is cool, mix in both flours. Whisk eggs and add to the mixture. Bake for 2 hours in a 7″ round tin.

V

Puteri mandi

Malayan

Ingredients
For dough balls
125g (1 cup) glutinous rice flour
pinch of salt

110ml (1/2 cup) water, to knead with flour

For sweet mixture
80g (3/4 cup) grated coconut
125ml (1/2 cup) coconut water
5g (1) Pandan (screwpine leaf)

50g (1/2 cup) palm sugar, cut coarsely

Method
For dough
Knead glutinous rice flour with 1/2 cup of water and pinch of salt. Divide the dough into marble size balls and flatten with thumb. Arrange in a container and set aside. Boil 2-3 cups of water in pot. Drop in the dough balls one at a time. In the meantime fill a bowl with cold water and put aside in readiness for the next step. When dough balls float up, remove with strainer and soak in cold water for a short time. Drain.

For sweet mixture
Cook palm sugar with coconut water. Once sugar has melted, add in grated coconut and screwpine leaf. Stir until slightly thickens. Add in the dough balls and mix well.
Remove and serve

Norul

V

Scottish shortbread

Scottish

Ingredients

6oz plain flour
2oz caster (granulated) sugar

4oz soft butter
1oz corn flour (cornstarch)

Method

Pre-heat oven to Gas mark 3 (325°F/170°C).
Mix the butter and sugar together (preferably with a wooden spoon) until it is pale and creamy. Sieve both the flour and the cornflour into the bowl and mix well. Put a small amount of flour on your working surface and place the dough on this. Shake a little flour on top and roll out to about quarter inch thick. Prick with a fork and cut into rounds with a cutter or, if you want one large shortbread round, pinch the edges with thumb and finger all round. Use a palette knife to lift the shortbread onto an oiled baking tray and bake for 25 minutes. If the biscuits are ready, they will be pale brown and crisp; if not, return to the oven for 5 or 10 minutes. Shake a small amount of caster/granulated sugar on the top of the shortbread immediately after they have been removed from the oven. Use a palette knife to move them to a cooling rack and store in an airtight tin once they are cold.

Shakira

V

Regular or special fruit cake

English

Ingredients

175g butter/margarine
3 eggs
225g plain flour
500g Fairtrade mixed fruit
1 tbsp milk

175g Fairtrade brown
caster sugar
Pinch of salt
Grated rind of 1 Fair Trade lemon

Method

Pre-heat oven to Gas mark 2 (300°F/150°C).
Cream the butter and sugar.
Beat in the eggs then fold in the flour, salt, fruit and lemon rind
Add milk and mix well. Bake in a greased, lined tin (7″ diameter
3″ high). Bake for 2 hours and 30 minutes.

For a special version, cover the cake, when quite cool, with
white icing and decorate with Fairtrade chocolate mini eggs.

Anne

V

Rhubarb & ginger jam

English Makes 4-5lbs

Ingredients
2 & 1/2 lbs prepared rhubarb
2 & 1/2 lbs sugar
1oz root ginger, bruised
4oz preserved or crystallised ginger, cut into small pieces

Method
Wipe and trim the rhubarb.
Put in a large heavy based pan and heat slowly, stirring continuously until boiling.
Add the sugar and the root ginger, tied in a muslin bag.
Boil rapidly for 15 minutes.
Remove the muslin bag and add the preserved or crystallised ginger.
Boil for a further 5 minutes or until the rhubarb is clear and setting point is reached.
Pot and cover in the usual way.

Sue

V

Sweet rice

Indian

Ingredients

2 cups jarda sugar
2 cups Basmati rice, washed
1 & 1/2 L water
2 cups of water to add to sugar

Optional
1 tbsp almonds blanched & chopped
1 tbsp pistachios, chopped

1/2 cup ghee or clarified butter
Pinch edible yellow colouring
or 3 strands saffron dissolved
in 1 tbsp of hot milk

Method

Boil the water and cook the rice for few minutes. Add a pinch of
edible yellow colouring, or saffron. Cook for another 5 minutes
(rice should be half cooked) and drain. Put ghee in a pot, add
sugar and water and let it boil until it is reduced by half. Add
half-cooked rice and cook on a very low heat for 15-20 minutes,
or until rice is cooked.Optional: Add chopped almonds,
pistachios and cardamom seeds to the rice.

Suhana Group

V

Sweet semolina

Turkish

Ingredients

1/2 kg semolina
1 packet unsalted butter/margarine
2 tbsp water

1/2 kg white sugar
1 L milk
200g pistachios
Pinch cinnamon powder

Method

Add the sugar to cold milk, mix well until all sugar is melted.
Crush the pistachios with a rolling pin into small pieces.
Melt the butter.
Add the semolina to the butter, stir and fry for 15 minutes on low heat, making sure that the semolina does not burn.
Add the sugared milk to the fried semolina, stirring continuously
When semolina starts to bubble, add the pistachios and turn the heat off.
Wash a flat tray and leave it wet, or pour 2 tablespoons of water on the tray. Pour the semolina mixture onto the tray, sprinkle cinnamon over the semolina and leave it to cool for 10 minutes.
When it is cold, put it in the fridge for 2 hours until the mixture is solid. When the mixture is cold and solid, take it out of the fridge. Slice to serve.

Serife

146

V

Yogurt cake

French

This sponge cake is so easy and simple. Its usually the first cake French children learn to bake. The pot containing the yogurt is used as a measure for the other ingredients.

Ingredients
1 pot of natural yogurt (125ml)
4 pots of flour
3 pots of sugar
2 pots of vegetable oil
4 eggs
1 tablespoon of baking powder

Method
Pre-heat the oven to Gas mark 6 (350°F/180°C).
Mix the flour, sugar and baking powder.
Add the eggs, oil and yogurt.
Pour into a baking tin (8") and bake for about 45 minutes.

This cake can be filled or iced with any of your favourite flavours. You can also add slices of apple or pineapple to the mix before baking.

Virginie